Praise for *The Demon in Den*

"Ryszard Legutko is a prophet. He fought communism as a young man, and today, he fights communism's far more sophisticated successors. Anyone who wants to know how to read the signs of our times must first read Legutko. *The Demon in Democracy* is one of those rare books with the power to utterly change the way you see the world."

Rod Dreher, senior editor of *The American Conservative*,
author of *The Benedict Option*

"Ryszard Legutko has written the indispensable book about the current crisis of liberalism and the relationship of liberalism to democracy. Incisive and deeply learned, steeped in the history and thought of Europe, it has proven widely influential in America and beyond."

Adrian Vermeule, Ralph S. Tyler Professor of Constitutional Law,
Harvard Law School

"In this wonderfully thoughtful and provocative book, Ryszard Legutko defends the moral contents of life (among them the Church and religion, the nation, classical metaphysics, moral conservatism, and the family) against a destructive ideology that has usurped the name of democracy. In graceful and pungent prose, he shows that the health and well-being of democracy depends on these humanizing and ennobling contents of life that are threatened by a utopian and politically correct form of 'democracy.' This is the conundrum that Legutko's book explores. It is as relevant to the United States and Western Europe as it is to those in the former Soviet Bloc who are mistakenly trying to 'catch up' to a West that is in the process of losing its soul. This book deserves the widest readership."

Daniel J. Mahoney, Augustine Chair in Distinguished Scholarship,
Assumption College

"No one is better qualified, whether by practical experience of totalitarianism, historical knowledge or philosophical depth, than Ryszard Legutko to cast a cool, impartial and ironic eye on the condition of modern liberal democracy. Always readable, he manages to avoid complacency without surrendering to despair."

Anthony Daniels, author and contributing editor of *City Journal*

"Legutko's compact study of the totalitarian tendencies of modern democracy is a work of scintillating brilliance. Every page is brimming with insights that at first surprise, but once digested, strike one as obvious. Legutko is a deeply learned but accessible guide through the apparent contradictions of liberalism's assault on liberty, democracy's dismissiveness toward ordinary people, and the anti-politics of a world obsessed by politics. I underlined most of the book upon first reading, and have underlined nearly all the rest during several re-readings. It is the most insightful work of political philosophy during this still young, but troubled century."

Patrick J. Deneen, David A. Potenziani Associate Professor of Political Science,
University of Notre Dame

The Demon in Democracy
Totalitarian Temptations in Free Societies

Ryszard Legutko

Translated by Teresa Adelson

Encounter Books
New York • London

First American edition published in 2016 by Encounter Books,
an activity of Encounter for Culture and Education, Inc.,
a nonprofit, tax exempt corporation.
Encounter Books website address: www.encounterbooks.com

Manufactured in the United States and printed on
acid-free paper. The paper used in this publication meets
the minimum requirements of ANSI/NISO Z39.48-1992
(R 1997) (*Permanence of Paper*).

First paperback edition published in 2018.
Paperback edition ISBN: 978-1-59403-991-1

THE LIBRARY OF CONGRESS HAS CATALOGUED
THE HARDCOVER EDITION AS FOLLOWS:

Names: Legutko, Ryszard, 1949– author.
Title: The demon in democracy : totalitarian temptations in free societies /
     by Ryszard Legutko.
Other titles: Triumf czlowieka pospolitego. English
Description: New York : Encounter Books, [2016] | "The book first appeared in
     Polish under the title *Triumf czlowieka pospolitego* (ZYSK 2012), and the
     present English translation (by Teresa Adelson and the author) is a
     slightly shortened and somewhat modified version of the original.—Title
     page verso. | Includes bibliographical references and index.
Identifiers: LCCN 2015044482 (print) | LCCN 2016004210 (ebook) | ISBN
     9781594038631 (hardcover : alk. paper) | ISBN 9781594038648 (Ebook)
Subjects: LCSH: Democracy—Philosophy. | Communism—Philosophy. | Comparative
     government.
Classification: LCC JC423 .L43413 2016 (print) | LCC JC423 (ebook) | DDC
     321.8—dc23
LC record available at http://lccn.loc.gov/2015044482

Interior page design and page composition by: BooksByBruce.com

Contents

FOREWORD / vii

INTRODUCTION / 1

CHAPTER I

History / 11

CHAPTER II

Utopia / 43

CHAPTER III

Politics / 73

CHAPTER IV

Ideology / 113

CHAPTER V

Religion / 145

CONCLUSION / 177

I think then that the species of oppression by which democratic nations are menaced is unlike anything which ever before existed in the world. I am trying myself to choose an expression which will accurately convey the whole of the idea I have formed of it, but in vain . . . I seek to trace the novel features under which despotism may appear in the world. The first thing that strikes the observation is an innumerable multitude of men all equal and alike, incessantly endeavoring to procure the petty and paltry pleasures with which they glut their lives. . . . Above this race of men stands an immense and tutelary power, which takes upon itself alone to secure their gratifications, and to watch over their fate. That power is absolute, minute, regular, provident and mild. It would be like the authority of a parent, if, like that authority, its object was to prepare men for manhood; but it seeks on the contrary to keep them in perpetual childhood; it is well content that the people should rejoice, provided they think of nothing but rejoicing.

ALEXIS DE TOCQUEVILLE, *DEMOCRACY IN AMERICA*

I have found from many observations that our liberals are incapable of allowing anyone to have his own convictions and immediately answer their opponent with abuse or something worse.

FYODOR DOSTOYEVSKY, *THE IDIOT*

That rabble had a mighty power over minds, for when the Lord God sends punishment on a nation he first deprives its citizens of reason. And so the wiser heads dared not resist the fops, and the whole nation feared them as some pestilence, for within itself it already felt the germs of disease. They cried out against the dandies but took pattern by them; they changed faith, speech, laws, and costumes. That was a masquerade, the licence of the Carnival season, after which was soon to follow the Lent of slavery.

ADAM MICKIEWICZ, *PAN TADEUSZ*

FOREWORD

In the first few pages of this important book, Ryszard Legutko describes the oddity whereby former communists adapted far more easily and successfully than former dissidents and anticommunists to the new liberal-democratic regimes established in Central and Eastern Europe after the fall of the Berlin Wall in 1989. Others have noticed this phenomenon too, but they have usually attributed it to such reasons as the former communists' having greater administrative experience, or the rules of "transition" protecting their power temporarily, or that, having privatized state enterprises into their own hands, they brought more resources to playing the game of politics in media and government.

These practical factors were certainly important. But they did not explain why there was so little *moral* resistance to the continuing dominance of the old *nomenklaturas* in post-communist democracies. Quite the contrary. Lightly rebaptized as social or liberal democrats, they dominated debate and formed governments. In Western Europe, public and private institutions, including European Union bodies, seemed to find former communists more congenial than former dissidents as partners in politics and business. On the rare occasions when resistance did erupt, it was usually in response to official efforts to expose still-influential communist networks, notably in intelligence agencies, or to restore state property to its original and rightful owners. It was almost as if anticommunist democrats were seen as a greater threat to the new liberal-democratic regime than those who had been its open enemies only the day before. In addition to their practical advantages, therefore, the former communists enjoyed a mysterious ideological edge.

Professor Legutko is both a prominent Polish and European statesman and a distinguished philosopher who, in addition to more conventional credentials, was once the editor of Solidarity's underground philosophy journal—a position that would have delighted G. K. Chesterton, as well as demonstrating the professor's devotion to truth and freedom. So he is ideally equipped to analyze the mystery of this ideological edge. He finds it in an unexpected place, namely in the structure and practices of the dominant political philosophy of the modern West: liberal democracy. This is a startling discovery. It surprised Legutko himself, and he is at pains to point out that, even with all the flaws he identifies, liberal democracy is manifestly superior humanly and politically to all forms of totalitarianism.

That said, he is able to demonstrate that liberal democracy, as it has developed in recent decades, shares a number of alarming features with communism. Both are utopian and look forward to "an end of history" where their systems will prevail as a permanent status quo. Both are historicist and insist that history is inevitably moving in their directions. Both therefore require that all social institutions—family, churches, private associations—must conform to liberal-democratic rules in their internal functioning. Because that is not so at present, both are devoted to social engineering to bring about this transformation. And because such engineering is naturally resisted, albeit slowly and in a confused way, both are engaged in a never-ending struggle against enemies of society (superstition, tradition, the past, intolerance, racism, xenophobia, bigotry, etc., etc.) In short, like Marxism before it, liberal democracy is becoming an all-encompassing ideology that, behind a veil of tolerance, brooks little or no disagreement.

This must strike a newcomer to the argument as absurd. But in chapter after chapter—on history, politics, religion, education, ideology—the author lays out strong evidence that this transformation is taking place. And transformation is the correct term. The regime described here by Legutko is not liberal democracy as it was understood by, say, Winston Churchill or FDR or John F. Kennedy or Ronald Reagan. That was essentially majoritarian democracy resting on constitutional liberal guarantees of free speech, free association, free media, and other liberties needed to ensure that debate was real and elections fair. Legutko hyphenates "liberal-democratic" as an adjective in the book; maybe he should do the same with the noun "liberal-democracy" to distinguish it from the liberal democracy of the nineteenth and twentieth centuries.

One of the most crucial differences between these two regimes is openness. Liberal democracy is a set of rules designed to ensure that government rests on the consent of the governed. Except within the broadest limits, it does not inherently dictate what policies should emerge from government or what social arrangements should be tolerated or prohibited. It is open to a wide range of policy outcomes and willing to accept a genuine diversity of social arrangements, including traditional ones. Here the people rule both as voters and as citizens making free choices. Liberal-democracy, however, has policies and prohibitions built into its ideological structure. It is not really open to institutions and policies that run counter to its "liberationist" instincts. It increasingly restricts their freedom to maneuver on anything from parental rights to national sovereignty. It is even hostile to some fundamental values of liberalism such as free speech. Accordingly it sometimes comes up against the wishes of the voters expressed in elections and referenda.

That is where the second crucial difference between liberal democracy and liberal-democracy enters the equation. In the former, the wishes of the majority, albeit qualified by negative constitutional restraints, ultimately determine law and policy. In the latter, policy is determined both by electoral majorities in accountable bodies and by a range of nonaccountable institutions such as courts that make laws rather than interpret them, transnational institutions such as the EU, UN treaty-monitoring bodies, and domestic bureaucracies with wide regulatory powers under delegated legislation. Increasingly, power has drained from elected bodies to courts and other nonaccountable institutions, the former have lost confidence, and the latter have become bolder, not merely restraining the majority but also dictating law and policy. The imperfect balance that has always existed within liberal democracy between democracy and liberalism has tipped heavily in favor of liberalism. Liberal-democracy is the result.

Paradoxically this is both less liberal and less democratic than liberal democracy. The range of acceptable political expression and the ability of voters to choose between different policies have both been greatly narrowed. In return, the voters have become increasingly alienated and inclined to rebel against the new structures of power. As all these outcomes become clearer, there will be a major debate in the Western democracies on the legitimacy of their governing institutions. When that debate happens—and it is already in train—this culturally rich, philosophically sophisticated, and brilliantly argued book will be an essential guide to understanding where we went wrong and how we can go right.

JOHN O'SULLIVAN
Editor-at-Large, *National Review*,
and Vice President and Executive Editor,
Radio Free Europe/Radio Liberty

INTRODUCTION

This book is about the similarities between communism and liberal democracy. The idea that such similarities exist started germinating timidly in my mind back in the Seventies of the last century, when for the first time I managed to get out of communist Poland to travel to the so-called West. To my unpleasant surprise, I discovered that many of my friends who consciously classified themselves as devoted supporters of liberal democracy—of a multiparty system, human rights, pluralism, and everything that every liberal democrat proudly listed as his acts of faith—displayed extraordinary meekness and empathy toward communism. I was unpleasantly surprised because it seemed to me that every liberal democrat's natural and almost visceral response to communism should be that of forthright condemnation.

For a while I thought that this anti-anticommunism, which was characterized by a lenient stance toward communists and a hard one against anticommunists, stemmed from the fear of the Soviets' power, or, to express it more graciously, from recognition that it was morally unthinkable to accept the possibility of a global military conflict as the inevitable consequence of a confrontation with communism. I realized, however, that such considerations did not fully explain the raw anti-anticommunist rage I perceived, which exceeded most negative political emotions known to me. A hypothesis came to my mind that both attitudes—the communist and the liberal-democratic—are linked by something more profound, some common principles and ideals.

Before long, however, this thought seemed to be so extravagant that I did not find enough inner strength or knowledge to explore it more deeply. What is more, at that time, from the perspective of someone like myself, a resident of the Soviet bloc, the West was the best of all possible worlds. Comparing it with communism smacked of blasphemy. The writings of the mostly left-wing authors who made such comparisons, such as Herbert Marcuse, elicited a strong antagonistic reflex among anticommunist Poles and were perceived as an offence to common sense and elementary decency. We treated the procommunist sympathies in Western societies as an accident rather than a fundamental defect.

I experienced the same budding thought for the second time during Poland's postcommunist period, right at the very beginning of its existence in 1989. Anti-anticommunism was activated simultaneously with the rise of the new liberal-democratic system (although to me and many of my friends, Poland seemed to be the last place on earth to harbor such ideas), and was almost immediately recognized as an important component of the new political orthodoxy that was taking shape. Those who were anticommunists were a threat to liberal democracy; those who were anti-anticommunist passed the most important and the most difficult entrance examination to the new political reality. These were the times when the communists were destroying the archives containing information of their activities and leaped forth to associate themselves with the new political and economic establishment from a much better position than the rest of us; and yet every negative word one uttered about them was not only stigmatized as villainy, but actually viewed as an attack on the best of the political systems to which we were humble newcomers.

The newly created Polish political elite embraced the communists with a show of impressive hospitality in part for tactical reasons (in order not to leave a large group of people outside the system), but also in no small part for ideological reasons: they predicted that following some slight touch-ups and finding themselves in new circumstances, the communists would become loyal and enthusiastic players in the liberal-democratic game. I quickly realized that this ideological assumption was true. Indeed, following some slight touch-ups and finding themselves in new circumstances, the former members of the Communist Party adapted themselves perfectly to liberal democracy, its mechanisms, and the entire ideological interpretation that accompanied these mechanisms. Soon they even joined the ranks of the guardians of the new orthodoxy. The same newspapers that for decades, on their front pages, had exhorted the proletarians of the world to unite began, with an equal zeal, to call on all enlightened forces to defend liberal democracy against the forces of darkness, including the anticommunists.

The fierce defense of the communists who were absorbed into the new system and the violent attacks on those whose opinion of their co-optation was far from enthusiastic, led many to believe that this was indeed the moral necessity of the new times. The communists who transformed themselves into the liberal democrats were considered trustworthy partners in the task of creating a new system, and an alliance with them was called an epoch-making contract, comparable in Polish history to the founding of the Republic in the history of the United States. Hence, the otherwise incomprehensible reaction of rage against the men of little faith who, like me, questioned the moral and political credibility of the newly co-opted partners. The rage still continues. It is symptomatic that in the history of the postcommunist societies the greatest political and journalistic hatchet jobs were against those who had doubts about granting the communists first immunity, then privileges.

The new system began to show symptoms that most political analysts ignored and that some, including myself, found most disturbing. When I talk about the system, I do not solely, or even mostly, mean an institutional structure, but everything that makes this structure function as it does: ideas, social practices, mores, people's attitudes. Communism and liberal democracy proved to be all-unifying entities compelling their followers how to think, what to do, how to evaluate events, what to dream, and what language to use. They both had their orthodoxies and their models of an ideal citizen.

Few people today doubt that communism was such an integrated political, ideological, intellectual, and sociolinguistic unity. Living in that system meant that one had to obey the minute directives of the ruling party to the extent that one was expected to become indistinguishable in words, thoughts, and deeds from millions of fellow citizens—Stalin's Russia, Mao's China, communist Albania, and North Korea being the closest approximations to the ideal. As for liberal democracy, the belief still lingers that it is a system of breathtaking diversity. But this belief has deviated from reality so much that the opposite view seems now closer to the truth. Liberal democracy is a powerful unifying mechanism, blurring differences between people and imposing uniformity of views, behavior, and language.

At the beginning of the Nineties I discovered something that was not particularly difficult to discover at the time: namely, that the nascent liberal democracy significantly narrowed the area of what was permissible. Incredible as it may seem, the final year of the decline of communism had more of the spirit of freedom than the period after the establishment of the new order, which immediately put a stop to something that many felt strongly at that time and that, despite its elusiveness, is known to everybody who has an experience of freedom—a sense of having many doors open and many possibilities to pursue. Soon this sense evaporated, subdued by the new rhetoric of necessity that the liberal-democratic system brought with itself. It did not take me long to make another, more depressing discovery: that this unifying tendency was not limited to the postcommunist world, and did not result from its peculiarities. Its adverse effects one could see throughout western civilization.

My subsequent experience of working in the European Parliament only endorsed my diagnosis. While there, I saw up close what—from a distance—escapes the attention of many observers. If the European Parliament is supposed to be the emanation of the spirit of today's liberal democracy, then this spirit is certainly neither good nor beautiful: it has many bad and ugly features, some of which, unfortunately, it shares with the spirit of communism. Even a preliminary contact with the EU institutions allows one to feel a stifling atmosphere typical of a political monopoly, to see the destruction of language turning into a new form of Newspeak, to observe the creation of a surreality, mostly ideological, that obfuscates the real world, to witness an uncompromising hostility against all dissidents, and to perceive many other things only too familiar to anyone who remembers the world governed by the Communist Party.

Interestingly this association with communism can quite often be heard in private conversations conducted in the EP corridors, even among loyal EU devotees. While annoyed with this system, they still do not challenge its fundamental rightness, probably hanging onto the belief that its disagreeable qualities are superficial and will, they hope, disappear with time. And they do not ask themselves, at least not openly, whether by any chance what annoys them is not the core of the system and consequently whether all these bad things half-jokingly referred to as Sovietlike will not intensify rather than disappear.

Similar thoughts are being disqualified by a seemingly irrefutable argument. How can one possibly compare the two systems, one of which was criminal, while the other, in spite of all the objections, gives people a lot of freedom and institutional protection? Surely, the difference between the Polish People's Republic and the democratic republic of today is so vast that only an insane person would deny it. In today's Poland, not communist any more, we have different political parties, the censorship office no longer exists, and economic freedom, despite various limitations, is much more advanced than during the communist rule. East Europeans travel without restrictions; they became part of the European Union and NATO and encounter no difficulties when establishing associations and organizations. The advantages of the modern democratic republic over the PPR are so obvious that only a person of bad faith could fail to see them. To give a personal argument for the superiority of one system over the other: in the Polish People's Republic the author of this book would have had neither a chance to write officially what he wrote in the democratic Poland, nor to serve in the public offices he held after the fall of the former regime.

This argument in such a formulation is, of course, irrefutable and no reasonable person would question it. But at the same time what it says should not be used in the function of an intellectual and moral blackmail. Whatever fundamental differences exist between the two systems, it is perfectly legitimate to ask why there are also some similarities, and why they are so profound and becoming more so. One cannot dismiss them with an argument that because the liberal-democratic system as such is clearly superior to communism, the existing similarities are absolved or explained away by the mere fact of this superiority. Because the liberal democrats are so fond of warning against all sorts of dangers that might undermine their political order, even if these are only suspected and felt rather than actually perceived (xenophobia, nationalism, intolerance, bigotry), one wonders why these same people completely ignore dangers that are easy to spot, namely, the increasing presence of developments similar to those that existed in the communist societies. Why do so few sound the alarm, even a bit prematurely, while trumpeting thousands of other dangers that are indiscernible even to the most trained eye?

The simplest answer is that there is some interplay between liberal democracy and communism. This book explains this interplay in detail. At the onset, I will point to one obvious link. Both communism and liberal democracy are regimes whose intent is to change reality for the better. They are—to use the current jargon—modernization projects. Both are nourished by the belief that the world cannot be tolerated as it is and that it should be changed: that the old should be replaced with the new. Both systems strongly and—so to speak—impatiently intrude into the social fabric and both justify their intrusion with the argument that it leads to the improvement of the state of affairs by "modernizing" it.

This word has a very peculiar connotation, initially stemming from technology because technology is and has always been about constant improvement. The language of modernization, by referring, if only associatively, to technology compels us to see the world as an object of engineering and innovative activity, almost like a machine to be improved by new devices and perfected by new inventions. The word "technology" comes, of course, from the Greek *technê*, which, as the ancients said, had such a powerful potential that it could make men equal to gods. It was Prometheus who made a gift of *technê* to the human race, the gift that enabled people to survive and then to improve their living conditions and make life better. This wonderful gift had, however, another side to it: the ancients warned that *technê* could, precisely because of its miraculous, almost divine creative potential, draw man into the sin of hubris.

Modernity made Prometheus a hero, and his gift was thought to be the best thing that ever happened to mankind because it was believed to be a vehicle of infinite progress carrying the human genius to unimaginable achievements. The meaning of modernization in today's world goes far beyond technology in standard terms, but the faith in it draws its strength largely from the unprecedented technological successes that man has achieved so far and with which it can yet surprise the world in the future.

The concept of modernization also brings with it the idea of breaking from the old and initiating the new. Although the word itself, through its imperfective form, assumes a graduated process (constant modernizing, not having something modernized once and for all), in its deeper layer it refers to Modernity, a completely new era that was born when its makers decided to reject everything that preceded it and to start anew. The creators of modernity—Machiavelli, Hobbes, and Bacon—saw themselves as pioneers of the new who boldly turned their backs on the past. Toward that past they felt, on the one hand, contempt of the kind one feels toward something both foolish and harmful, and on the other hand, sympathy mixed with the condescension one may feel toward something that had once, perhaps, some nobility and charm, but which disappeared, never to return. Even if some of the modernizers took advantage of the old—and many did—they, like Descartes, did so without admitting it, and did all they could to obliterate any traces of inspiration. *Modernitas* thus inevitably involves conscious detachment, passing over the border, crossing the Rubicon, severing the umbilical cord, growing up and leaving adolescence behind, and doing other similar things denoted by dozens of other more or less platitudinous metaphors.

"Modernization" also implies experiencing something refreshing and invigorating in human relations and in social and political arrangements: greater freedom, openness, and lightness of existence. Although in the modernized world technology is becoming more advanced and institutions more complex, modern human life returns to what is simple and elementary. People cast off unnecessary corsets, masks, postures, and costumes. They are once again young, optimistic, straightforward, and liberated, like the unforgettable Youngbloods family from Witold Gombrowicz's *Ferdydurke*. The feeling of guilt, metaphysical or religious, disappears, together with irrational moral and psychological barriers that were built on this feeling. Old obligations fade, and modern man acts more and more on his own account with a proud sense of individual independence and sovereignty. But at the same time—which may seem paradoxical but is not—considering himself detached from any obligations, he increasingly cultivates the belief that his affirming individual independence and sovereignty is a step on the road to a better world for the entire human race. Thus by considering himself as being separate, he exults in the belief—hidden deep in his heart—that he is a participant, together with millions of others like himself, in a march toward the future.

When we look at communism and liberal democracy from this point of view, we can see that they are both fuelled by the idea of modernization. In both systems a cult of technology translates itself into acceptance of social engineering as a proper approach to reforming society, changing human behavior, and solving existing social problems. This engineering may have a different scope and dynamics in each case, but the society and the world at large are regarded as undergoing a continuous process of construction and reconstruction. In one system this meant reversing the current of Siberia's rivers, in the other, a formation of alternative family models; invariably, however, it was the constant improvement of nature, which turns out to be barely a substrate to be molded into a desired form. Although today's ideology of environmentalism fashioned idolatrous reverence for the earth and its fauna and flora, it did not change the enthusiasm for treating human nature and society in a dangerously technological manner.

Both regimes clearly distance themselves from the past. Both embrace the idea of progress with all its consequences, being a natural offshoot of the belief in the power of *technê*. In both whatever happens is assessed with respect to its relation to the old or the new. Having the brand of the new is always preferable; being with the old is always suspect. The favorite expressions of condemnation always point to the old: "superstition," "medieval," "backward," and "anachronistic"; the favorite adulatory term is, of course, "modern." It goes without saying that everything—in both communism and liberal democracy—should be modern: thinking, family, school, literature, and philosophy. If a thing, a quality, an attitude, an idea is not modern, it should be modernized or will end up in the dustbin of history (an unforgettable expression having as much relevance for the communist ideology as for the liberal-democratic). This was a reason why the former communists, who for so many decades had been fighting for progress against the forces of backwardness, so quickly found allies in liberal democracy, where the struggle for progress animates practically every aspect of individual and collective activities, progress is largely in the same direction, and backwardness is represented by the same forces.

Both systems generate—at least in their official ideological interpretations—a sense of liberation from the old bonds. By becoming a member of a communist and liberal-democratic society, man rejects a vast share of loyalties and commitments that until not long ago shackled him, in particular those that were imposed on him through the tutelage of religion, social morality, and tradition. He feels renewed and strong and therefore has nothing but pity toward those miserable ones who continue to be attached to long-outdated rules and who succumb to the bondage of unreasonable restraints. But there is one obligation from which he cannot be relieved: for a communist, communism, and for a liberal democrat, liberal democracy. These obligations are non-negotiable. Others can be ignored.

Having cast away the obligations and commitments that come from the past, the communist and the liberal democrat quickly lose their memory of it or, alternatively, their respect for it. Both want the past eradicated altogether or at least made powerless as an object of relativizing or derision. Communism, as a system that started history anew, had to be, in essence and in practice, against memory. Those who were fighting the regime were also fighting for memory against forgetting, knowing very well that the loss of memory strengthened the communist system by making people defenseless and malleable. There are no better illustrations of how politically imposed amnesia helps in the molding of the new man than the twentieth-century anti-utopias *1984* and *Brave New World*. The lessons of Orwell and Huxley were, unfortunately, quickly forgotten. In my country at the very moment when communism fell and the liberal-democratic order was emerging, memory again became one of the main enemies. The apostles of the new order lost no time in denouncing it as a harmful burden hampering striving for modernity. In this anti-memory crusade, as in several other crusades, they have managed to be quite successful, more so than their communist predecessors.

This book will examine these and other similarities between communism and liberal democracy in detail. It will also address the questions that must be asked as soon as the similarities are identified: first, whether an underlying cause exists that makes these two systems, seemingly so different, tend to resemble each other, and second, what conclusions follow for those of us who have lived in the present system, proudly called a Western democracy, for more than two decades, but who have not forgotten what it meant to live under a communist dictatorship.

CHAPTER I

★ ☭ ★

History

★ 1 ★

Let us begin with what seems obvious: that communism and liberal democracy share a similar perception of history. Societies—as the supporters of the two regimes are never tired of repeating—are not only changing and developing according to a linear pattern but also improving, and the most convincing evidence of the improvement, they add, is the rise of communism and liberal democracy. And even if a society does not become better at each stage and in each place, it should continue improving given the inherent human desire to which both regimes claim to have found the most satisfactory response.

The communist view of history is well-known. The simplest version, the one that circulated among the great unwashed in people's democracies, was that communism is bound to prevail everywhere, even in the capitalist United States, among our distant African comrades, and on any other continent. In its Marxian version, this was expressed in a more complex way. Marx and his colleagues did not occupy themselves with communism as the goal of history and did not deliberate over details of the communist political machines to be. Such a prospect was too fanciful and vague. What they focused on was an analysis of capitalism and the transition from the present to the future system.

The description of the historical process leading to communism has three main versions. According to the first, socialism/communism was the final stage of social development, illuminated by the discovery of Marx's laws of history. As Engels famously said at Marx's funeral, just as Darwin discovered the laws of nature, so Marx discovered the law governing societies. According to these inexorable and universally binding laws, capitalism would be superseded by socialism due to the inherent logic of history, just as in nature some species had replaced others as a result of innate processes of natural selection. Later on, the liberals sharply attacked this view. Karl Popper, to give the best known example, argued in his books on historicism and totalitarianism that history cannot be an object of a scientific inquiry and therefore it is impossible to discover the laws of historical development. In fact, he said more than that. He claimed that those who, like communists, formulate such laws not only commit a methodological mistake but also open up the field for political violence, which they feel free to use in the name of the future.

In communist countries, historical thinking translated itself into a very simplistic, but politically momentous formula. Communism would prevail everywhere—it was said—but there were countries that were more or less advanced on their road to it. The most advanced was, of course, the Soviet Union. The orthodox disciples of the laws of history thus surmised that all other countries would have to advance through the same stages that the Soviet Union did. Later on, this doctrinaire assumption was modified to allow for some national specificities, which were called the Polish, or the Romanian, or the Hungarian roads to communism. The idea of national specificity of communism came to be more or less adopted in practice, but never in the official ideology, because it could have legitimized the unthinkable and unpardonable act of leaving "the Socialist Camp." (This expression is not the author's irony, but the term then officially used.)

The second version of the transition from capitalism to communism was through a conscious human action: the society could be pushed forward to the next stage of development by the group that was most aware of its historical role. Who this group was supposed to be was a hotly discussed issue. The most common response was, of course, the proletariat. Another possibility was the Communist Party, which was believed to be the vanguard of the proletariat. Some pointed out the peasants, as in China, where there was no industry and, therefore, no working class; others—as in the 1968 revolution that shook the Western world—students and intellectuals. The constitutions of the people's democracies ascribed this role to the "working people of town and country," which in practice meant, of course, the Communist Party.

The third idea for the transition to communism, the most complex and the most difficult to translate into political categories, originated from specific anthropological assumptions, according to which the historical development of humanity was toward full self-consciousness, which meant the full realization of human nature. Leszek Kołakowski, in his history of Marxism, made this insight, which he derived from earlier philosophical sources, the key to understanding the whole Marxist tradition. Thus the quest for communism was not dictated solely by implementing a specific political plan or simply by a desire to win the power struggle for social justice. All of these strategies sprang from a deeper source, which was to bring the human potential to its full flourishing.

This humanistic-anthropological theory, somewhat convoluted and expressed in an unintelligible language of German metaphysics, was to play a significant role in the history of Marxism. It was dug up from time to time, especially in the twentieth century, when communism transformed itself into a regime of crime and terror, in order to rehabilitate the movement's human face and to contrast it—in its refined anthropology—with Bolshevik socialism. The humanistic thrust was associated with the young Marx's remaining under the influence of Hegel and contrasted with the old Marx, Engels, and Lenin, and, indirectly, with the Soviet Union and communist parties, over which—as it was argued—the spirits of the old Marx, Engels, and Lenin presided.

These three scenarios were not separated by Karl Marx but constituted the three aspects of the same historical process. There existed laws of history—the laws that were objectively determining the direction of historical change. These were executed through human activities by groups and organizations such as communist parties that were increasingly aware of their historical roles; all of this contributed to the growing self-consciousness of humanity on its road to the fullness of existence. Needless to say, in the communist practice, the unity of the three aspects did not matter because the interpretation of historicism depended not on the choice of a philosophy but on the current party line.

The concept of communism as the culmination of history was not a mere succession of political regimes. History covered the entirety of human experience including human nature, the human mind, social relations, law, institutions, and even science and art. The group that took responsibility for change was clearly, at the beginning, a partisan group, almost marginal in the context of the then-existing political system, but in the process of approaching the final stage of history, was growing in importance, and finally became the only political actor capable of pulling together and transforming—whether gradually or radically, peacefully or by force—everyone and everything, thus elevating the human species to new, previously unknown levels. A segment, party, or faction from some point in history was granted the status of the midwife and architect of the whole: in the short stretch, of one society (Russian, Polish, German), and in the long haul, of the whole of humanity.

From the perspective of historicism any opposition to this process was extremely harmful to humanity and inconceivably stupid. What the enemy of progress defended was by definition hopelessly parochial, limited to one class, decadent, anachronistic, historically outdated, and degenerate; sooner or later it had to give way to something that was universal, necessary, and inclusive of the whole of humanity. It was obvious to any open mind that history had to grant victory to communists and that all they had to do was to wait patiently for the signs of impending victory. Communist artists and intellectuals produced countless treatises, novels, films, and plays showing how the new times condemned the enemies of communism to the dustbin of history and how the armies of socialism marched to their final factory. For an average citizen of a communist country it was enough to take a look at a newspaper or turn on the radio to be convinced of this implacable truth.

And yet despite the ardent belief in historical inevitability, the longtime prospect of the advent of socialism for the entire human race at some point drifted far away, so far that it ceased to be seriously taken into consideration. History might indeed eventually admit that communism was right, but the signs of its conquests were increasingly weaker; the world revolution was not coming and, in fact, was not even close. The failure of spreading the flame of the Bolshevik revolution to Western Europe closed a certain chapter in the communist narrative.

The idea of bestowing the blessings of communism on all people on earth was thus abandoned. Instead, the Party doubled its efforts in the countries that were lucky enough to find themselves in a communist orbit. The success of the new order depended on the rate and extent of penetration of communism in all areas of life. In more concrete terms, it meant, among other things, that the entire society had to be transformed into a communist society, with all communities and institutions controlled by the Communist Party, the sole maker and arbiter of socialist standards. We in Poland had a socialist society, socialist schools and universities, a socialist family, socialist morality, and, for some time, even socialist art and socialist realism. In the socialist motherland we had the socialist economy in which people worked in a system that took the form of a socialist competition.

What did such language mean in practice? First of all, it was a signal that everything and everyone was involved in "building socialism" and that it was not possible to evade this task; the person who dodged the duty could reasonably be suspected of stupidity or bad intentions, and usually of both. Even relatively independent organizations—and these were few—had to submit regular declarations to prove that they participated in work according to the best of their abilities and that they certainly appreciated the value of the project. Sometimes this meant—especially in the beginning—a radical restructuring that would change everything and not leave anything as it was before. Such was the experience of the universities, schools, and all organizations that, when restructured in accordance with the nature of the communist system, lost their heritage and acquired a new function and a new identity.

For a long time, building socialism was presented as a race against capitalism and bourgeois society; the more socialist we made ourselves, the less we were capitalist-bourgeois, and thus our ranking in the race improved. Later on, the race rhetoric subsided because of the leadership's weakened self-confidence and the decreasing chances of success. What remained, however, was a habit, even though only verbal, to oppose all that was capitalist and bourgeois, because—and this message was transmitted with paralyzing monotony—communism in one form or another was our destiny. For all of us living in the "camp of socialist countries," history was already determined. The reconstruction of the old bourgeois structures could not be expected because the eggs from which the omelet was made had disappeared long ago. Rather, one had to look for a place in the new communist structures and adapt them to the elementary requirements of reason. Even if capitalist-bourgeois elements were to appear from time to time as necessary concessions in order to save the country from a dramatic disaster, they still had to have a socialist label.

★ 2 ★

Liberal democracy does not have and never had an official concept of history that can be attributed to a particular author. It does not have its Marx, Lenin, or Lukács. Nevertheless, from the very beginning, the liberals and the democrats made use of a typical historical pattern by which they were easily recognized and which often appeared not only in the variety of general opinions they formulated but also, on a less abstract level, in popular beliefs and stereotypes professed to be a representation of liberal thinking in mass circulation. According to this view, the history of the world—in the case of liberalism—was the history of the struggle for freedom against enemies who were different at various stages of history but who perpetually fought against the idea of freedom itself and—in the case of democracy—the history of a people's continuing struggle for power against forces that kept them submissive for centuries. Both of these political currents—liberal and democratic—had therefore one enemy, a widely understood tyranny, which, in the long history of humanity, assumed a variety of additional, distinctive costumes. Every now and then it was a monarchy, often the Church, and at other times an oligarchy. The main enemy of freedom was portrayed in various ways in different countries and different traditions. As John Stuart Mill wrote in the passage opening his essay "On Liberty," "The struggle between Liberty and Authority is the most conspicuous feature of history since the earliest times known to us."

In England, at some point there emerged a Whig concept of history that was to portray the country's basic dramatic political history. According to this view, the history of British civilization was a progressing expansion of freedom and its legal safeguards and the disappearance into the past of bad practices of autocracy or arbitrary authority beyond the control of the people and Parliament. More specifically, the history of England could be presented—as has been done many times—as a narrative of the emergence of Parliament and creation of a constitutional monarchy, with a particular legal system sanctioning it.

But the Whig view of the history of Great Britain deserves a broader look. There were also authors who treated it as a basic libertarian model of development. If one was going to introduce the idea of freedom to Western civilization, then—as they claimed—the most clearly expressed representation of the idea of freedom at its most mature, the one most rooted in law, institutions, and customs and in freedom mechanisms themselves, was revealed in the history of England. Such were the feelings of numerous Anglophiles, from the Enlightenment thinkers to Friedrich Hayek.

Naturally, a question arises of what was supposed to happen and would happen at the end of history, when freedom would claim victory over tyranny. There, for millions of people, communism offered a rousing but actually quite vague vision. Under communism people were promised to have a lot of time off from work, to be free from alienation, to find employment that was rewarding and fulfilling, and to have the means of production socialized, which would result in each person receiving according to his needs. What all that was supposed to mean in more specific terms, nobody knew. When Soviet communism emerged, some said that in fact it was precisely the system that the socialist prophets had in mind; others categorically opposed this opinion, claiming that communism was a terrible perversion of genuine socialism, while still others argued that the Soviet regime was merely a transitional phase—somewhat unpleasant yet necessary, leading to the future realization of socialist ideals. Given the vague notions of what true socialism was supposed to be, each of these assessments was right to some extent.

The liberal vision, although less thrilling to hearts and minds, was a bit more concrete. The impetus of liberalism was understood to lie in its cooperative feature, which was to bring the human race to a higher stage of development, then called the Age of Commerce. The era of conflicts, wars, and violence—it was claimed—was coming to an end and the period of cooperation, prosperity, and progress was near. In short, the liberal era was the era of peace. This, in any case, was the way of think-ing one could find in Adam Smith, Frédéric Bastiat, and other classical liberals. It does not sound particularly grand or original today, but we should remember that war was a ubiquitous experience then, and thus the prospect of peace appeared tempting if almost unrealistic and the theories that justified it had to appear exciting in their boldness.

In a famous essay, Immanuel Kant wrote about the advent of the era of "perpetual peace" among the republics. What is interesting, however, is that, according to Kant, this blessed era could and actually should be preceded by a phase of enlightened absolutism. Authors such as Spinoza, who wrote favorably about democracy, made their praise conditional on people's first meeting high intellectual and moral requirements. They believed—and it was a fairly widespread view at the time—that tyranny, despotism, and other anachronistic regimes hindered the development of human capacity, stopping it at the early stages of dependency and helplessness. Following the removal of such regimes, work was to begin—partly resulting from spontaneous internal desire for self-improvement of the mind and partly imposed by the enlightened rulers—that in the end would generate an improved society composed of better and more rational individuals.

A comparison between the liberal-democratic concept of the history and that of communism shows a commonality of argument as well as of images of the historical process. Three common threads occurring in Marx's works have their counterparts in the liberal and democratic tra-dition. There is a belief in the unilateralism of history, leading inevitably and triumphantly to the era of perpetual peace, or, in other terms, to the refinement of commerce and cooperation that humanity will reach due to the victory of freedom over tyranny. Another is the equivalent of deliber-ate human action, albeit not run by the party, but by active entrepreneurs and all types of freedom fighters, as well as the distinguished minority groups, elite and enlightened rulers who will prepare humanity—until now apathetic, enslaved, and ignorant—for the new reality. The third topic—mankind's achieving maturity and intellectual independence—is usually described in simpler language than the German-Romantic used by the young Karl Marx and amounts to a promise of a modern society liberated from ignorance and superstition.

★ 3 ★

Over the past 150 or two hundred years the concepts of communism, liberalism, and democracy evolved under the pressures of reality. It seems beyond doubt, however, that the first two views—that history has a unilateral pattern and that a better world is shaped by conscious human activity—are still very much present in the modern political mind.

Of course, few people talk of the laws of history today, mainly because this quasi-scientific language lost its appeal in an age when the concept of science changed. Nevertheless, both the communists and liberal democrats have always upheld and continue to uphold the view that history is on their side. Whoever thought that the collapse of the Soviet system should have done away with the belief in the inevitability of socialism was disappointed. This belief is as strong as ever and the past practices of socialism—whether Soviet or Western—are well-appreciated, not because they were beneficial in themselves, but because they are still believed to have represented the correct direction of social change. One can observe a similar mindset among the liberal democrats, who are also deeply convinced that they represent both the inherent dynamics of social development and a natural tendency in human aspirations.

Both the communists and liberal democrats, while praising what is inevitable and objectively necessary in history, praise at the same time the free activities of parties, associations, community groups, and organizations in which, as they believe, what is inevitable and objectively necessary reveals itself. Both speak fondly of "the people" and large social movements, while at the same time—like the Enlightenment philosophers—have no qualms in ruthlessly breaking social spontaneity in order to accelerate social reconstruction.

Admittedly, for the liberal democrats, combination of the two threads is intellectually more awkward than for the socialists. The very idea of liberal democracy should presuppose the freedom of action, which means every man and every group or party should be given a free choice of what they want to pursue. And yet the letter, the spirit, and the practice of the liberal-democratic doctrine is far more restrictive: so long as society pursues the path of modernization, it must follow the path whereby the programs of action and targets other than liberal-democratic lose their legitimacy. The need for building a liberal-democratic society thus implies the withdrawal of the guarantee of freedom for those whose actions and interests are said to be hostile to what the liberal democrats conceive as the cause of freedom.

Thus the adoption of the historical preference of liberal democracy makes the resulting conclusion analogous to that which the communists drew from the belief in the historical privilege of their system: everything that exists in society must become liberal-democratic over time and be imbued with the spirit of the system. As once when all major designations had to be preceded by the adjective "socialist" or "communist," so now everything should be liberal, democratic, or liberal-democratic, and this labeling almost automatically gives a recipient a status of credibility and respectability. Conversely, a refusal to use such a designation or, even worse, a ostentatious rejection of it, condemns one to moral degradation, merciless criticism, and, ultimately, historical annihilation.

Countries emerging from communism provided striking evidence in this regard. Belief in the "normalcy" of liberal democracy, or, in other words, the view that this system delineates the only accepted course and method of organizing collective life, is particularly strong, a corollary being that in the line of development the United States and Western Europe are at the forefront while we, the East Europeans, are in the back. The optimal process should progress in a manner in which the countries in the back catch up with those at the front, repeating their experiences, implementing their solutions, and struggling with the same challenges. Not surprisingly, there immediately emerged a group of self-proclaimed eloquent *accoucheurs* of the new system, who from the position of the enlightened few took upon themselves a duty to indicate the direction of change and to infuse a new liberal-democratic awareness into anachronistic minds. They were, one would be tempted to say, the Kantian Prussian kings of liberal democracy, fortunately devoid of a comparable power, but undoubtedly perceiving themselves to have a similar role as pioneers of the enlightened future.

In their view, today also consciously or unconsciously professed by millions, the political system should permeate every section of public and private life, analogously to the view of the erstwhile *accoucheurs* of the communist system. Not only should the state and the economy be liberal, democratic, or liberal-democratic, but the entire society as well, including ethics and mores, family, churches, schools, universities, community organizations, culture, and even human sentiments and aspirations. The people, structures, thoughts that exist outside the liberal-democratic pattern are deemed outdated, backward-looking, useless, but at the same time extremely dangerous as preserving the remnants of old authoritarianisms. Some may still be tolerated for some time, but as anyone with a minimum of intelligence is believed to know, sooner or later they will end up in the dustbin of history. Their continued existence will most likely threaten the liberal-democratic progress and therefore they should be treated with the harshness they deserve.

Once one sends one's opponents to the dustbin of history, any debate with them becomes superfluous. Why waste time, they think, arguing with someone whom the march of history condemned to nothingness and oblivion? Why should anyone seriously enter into a debate with the opponent who represents what is historically indefensible and what will sooner or later perish? People who are not liberal democrats are to be condemned, laughed at, and repelled, not debated. Debating with them is like debating with alchemists or geocentrists. Again, an analogy with communism immediately comes to one's mind. The opponents of communism—e.g., those who believed free-market to be superior to planned economy—were at best enemies to be crushed, or laughingstocks to be humiliated: how else could any reasonable soul react to such anachronistic dangerous ravings of a deluded mind?

After all, in a liberal democracy everyone knows—and only a fool or a fanatic can deny—that sooner or later a family will have to liberalize or democratize, which means that the parental authority has to crumble, the children will quickly liberate themselves from the parental tutelage, and family relationships will increasingly become more negotiatory and less authoritarian. These are the inevitable consequences of the civilizational and political development, giving people more and more opportunities for independence; moreover, these processes are essentially beneficial because they enhance equality and freedom in the world. Thus there is no legitimate reason to defend the traditional family—the very name evokes the smell of mothballs—and whoever does it is self-condemned to a losing position and in addition perpetrates harm by delaying the process of change. The traditional family was, after all, part of the old despotism: with its demise the despotic system loses its base. The liberalization and democratization of the family are therefore to be supported—wholeheart-edly and energetically—mainly by appropriate legislation that will give children more power: for example, allowing increasingly younger girls to have abortions without parental consent, or providing children with legal instruments to combat their claims against their parents, or depriving parents of their rights and transferring those rights to the government and the courts. Sometimes, to be sure, these things can lead to excessive measures perpetrated by the state, law, and public opinion, but the general tendency is good and there is no turning back from it.

Similarly, in a liberal democracy everyone knows—and only a fool or a fanatic can deny—that schools have to become more and more lib-eral and democratic for the same reasons. Again, this inevitable process requires that the state, the law, and public opinion harshly counteract against all stragglers—those who are trying to put a stick in the spokes of progress, dreamers who imagine that in the twenty-first century we can return to the school as it existed in the nineteenth, pests who want to build an old-time museum in the forward-rushing world. And so on, and so forth. Similar reasoning can be applied to churches, communities, associations.

As a result, liberal democracy has become an all-permeating system. There is no, or in any case, cannot be, any segment of reality that would be arguably and acceptably non–liberal democratic. Whatever happens in school must follow the same pattern as in politics, in politics the same pattern as in art, and in art the same pattern as in the economy: the same problems, the same mechanisms, the same type of thinking, the same language, the same habits. Just as in real socialism, so in real democracy it is difficult to find some nondoctrinal slice of the world, a nondoctrinal image, narrative, tone, or thought.

In a way, liberal democracy presents a somewhat more insidious ideological mystification than communism. Under communism it was clear that communism was to prevail in every cell of social life, and that the Communist Party was empowered with the instruments of brutal coercion and propaganda to get the job done. Under liberal democracy such official guardians of constitutional doctrine do not exist, which, paradoxically, makes the overarching nature of the system less tan-gible, but at the same time more profound and difficult to reverse. It is the people themselves who have eventually come to accept, often on a preintellectual level, that eliminating the institutions incompatible with liberal-democratic principles constitutes a wise and necessary step.

Forty years ago, at the time when the period of liberal-democratic monopoly was fast approaching, Daniel Bell, one of the popular social writers, set forth the thesis that a modern society is characterized by the disjunction of three realms: social, economic, and political. They develop—so he claimed—at different rates, have different dynamics and purposes, and are subject to different mechanisms and influences. This image of structural diversity that Bell saw coming was attractive, or rather would have been attractive if true. But the opposite happened. No disjunction occurred. Rather, everything came to be joined under the liberal-democratic formula: the economy, politics and society, and—as it turns out—culture.

The very idea that political regimes come into being through historical necessity must seem dubious, not to say ludicrous, to any sane mind. Unquestionably, an infinite number of additional parameters, including yet-unknown and unexpected ones, may change the direction of history. Even if one is deeply attached to liberal democracy, one should always keep in mind that there are many worthy goals—inconsistent with the movement's mechanisms and traditions—that a lot of people can or should pursue, because they enrich our experience and have accompanied human strivings since time immemorial. Besides, once we grant—and the liberal democrats usually do—that progress has been made possible by mankind's incessant pursuit of creativity, inventiveness, power of imagination, and freedom of thought, and that these qualities have often changed the course of history, why should we all of a sudden acquiesce to a complacent notion that the same qualities cannot lead us beyond the liberal-democratic horizon?

The so-called Hegelian sting (or, to put it simply, veneration of historical necessity) has been well described, mainly by Czesław Miłosz in *The Captive Mind*, which analyzes mechanisms of the communist servility of Polish intellectuals. The author himself, let it be noted, was likewise massively stung and for the rest of his life struggled painfully with the vicissitudes of historicism, which he never entirely abandoned.

The manner of thinking that made artists and intellectuals kowtow to the communist creed and subsequently to invest all their intellectual and artistic capital to legitimize its atrocities, which Miłosz recreated accurately, captures an important—even if not the entire—aspect of the treason of the intelligentsia in totalitarian systems.

It seems that the idolatry of liberal democracy, which nowadays we observe among the same groups that so easily succumbed to a totalitarian temptation—their angry rejection of even the slightest criticism, their inadvertent acceptance of the obvious maladies of the system, their silencing of dissenters, their absolute support for the monopoly of one ideology and one political system—are part of the same disease to which, apparently, intellectuals and artists are particularly susceptible. It thus seems that the mental enslavement described by Miłosz was not a single occurrence occasioned by a short-lived infatuation with communism, but an inherent handicap of the modern mind.

One can imagine two opposing mindsets represented by two attitudes: that of an old man and that of a youngster. The old man, with his rich experience, is likely to be wary of further fundamental changes, perceiving them to be an ever-recurrent symptom of immaturity; the youngster, full of energy, will enthusiastically get involved in changing the world for the better according to the plan that he believes to be superior to all previous ones. The old man will prefer to remain meditative, prompting young people to learn from the older and wiser, calling for humility, prudence, and discretion; the youngster is active, happy to instruct others, full of pride in his responses, bold in action, dreaming of transgression and admiring it in others. The old man will be inclined to think that everything has already been done; the young man believes that he himself, society, and perhaps even humanity are currently facing a unique opportunity in history. The old man will be guided by the image of a golden age: everything used to be better until a lasting and deepening decline that most likely stems from corruption of human nature; the youngster looks into the future and believes that all the best things for the human race are yet to come and that the history of humanity, despite occasional calamities, shows a steady progress. The old man is balanced in his reactions and assessments, looking for the appropriate courses of action in the world, which, according to him, was founded on human error, ignorance, poor recognition of reality, and premature ventures; the youngster has an excitable nature, moving from desperation to euphoria, eagerly identifying numerous enemies whose destruction he volubly advocates, and equally happy to engage in collaborative activities with others, because—he believes—the world is full of rational people. The old man says that, given the weaknesses of the human race, institutions and communities (families, schools, churches) should be protected because over the centuries they have proven themselves to be tools to tame humans' evil inclinations; the young man will argue that such institutions and communities need to be radically exposed to light, aired out, and transformed because they are fossils of past injustices. The old man is a loner who believes that only such an attitude as his can protect the integrity of the mind; the youngster eagerly joins the herd, enjoying the uproar, mobilization, and direct action.

When, in the light of this dichotomy, we take a look at the modern mind, we might say—at the risk of simplification—that it resembles that of a youngster much more than that of an old man. This mind, equipped with a variety of assumptions and technical means, ventured a huge attempt to reform knowledge, society, and individual people. The most obvious of its assumptions is that the purpose of man's existence in the world is to change things. The youngster—relevant to his age—arms this assumption with arrogance, self-indulgence, and irresponsibility.

The socialist and a liberal-democratic interpretation of history is typical of a youngster's: it delivers the promise of a great transformation; it is bold, absolute, simplistic, easily stimulated by optimistic projects. It is only natural that so many intellectuals have been at the service of this promise at least since the Renaissance era, worshipping revolutions and plans for new ones. To the youngster, communism once presented itself as the greatest, most comprehensive and most sublime idea for such a transformation. Another idea at the time was fascism, which was close to socialism—in style, at least—and appeared in several national versions, of which the Italian interpretation won the greatest acclaim as a manifestation of youth.

The parliamentary systems were not so exalted. As part of various national traditions and institutions, they preserved their common sense and fared well at a time when half the world had gone mad for communism, fascism, and German National Socialism and surrendered to bloody excesses with the approval of the masses and a large part of the elites. At some point, however—when they became the model of "democracy" and "liberal democracy"—everything changed. Suddenly, it turned out that liberal democracy was the global pioneer of progress and that it, rather than its predecessors or competitors, was to bring humanity to a stage of development that had only been dreamed of for centuries.

An intellectual in a liberal democracy faces a similar dilemma to the one that once troubled his fellow socialist: whether to join the vast torrent of history or to remain on the sidelines, to continue to be a vigorous youngster transforming the world or to change into a grumpy old man who does not like much and whose wisdom has little social effect. For many, the choice turned out to be not so difficult after all. Moving with the flow—the socialist and liberal-democratic—gives an intellectual more power, or at least an illusion of it. He feels like a part of a powerful global machine of transformation. He not only understands the process of change better than others and knows how to organize the world, but also—by looking at the surrounding reality—can easily diagnose which phenomena, communities, and institutions will disappear and, when resisting, will have to be eliminated for the sake of the future. Therefore he reacts with indignant pity toward anyone who wants to stop the unstoppable. He indulges in a favorite occupation of the youngster: to criticize what is in the name of what will be, but what a large part of humanity, less perceptive and less intelligent than himself, fails to see.

The youngster committed to liberal democracy is, however, somewhat different from his communist comrade. Communism was entirely a figment of the imagination of theorists who put it to practice as a big and brutal experiment against the will of the majority, while liberal democracy is no invention, but a system that boasts an impressive track record and has grown out of the cumulative experience of generations. At a time when death camps, gulags, five-year plans, and political police regimes were created, many Western countries preserved that which is difficult to overestimate and always worth defending: parliamentarianism, a multiparty system, and the rule of law.

This youngster, however, fails to notice that at some point this system, or rather the arrangement of systems covering many variants, became haughty, dogmatic, and dedicated not so much to facilitating the resolution of political conflicts as to transforming society and human nature.

It lost its prior restraint and caution, created powerful tools to influence every aspect of life, and set in motion institutions and laws, frequently yielding to the temptation to conduct ideological warfare against disobedient citizens and groups. Falling into a trap of increasing self-glorification, the system began to define itself more and more against its supposed opposition, i.e., all sorts of nonliberal and nondemocratic enemies whose elimination was considered a necessary condition to achieve the next level of ideological purity. The multiparty system was gradually losing its pluralistic character, parliamentarianism was becoming a vehicle of tyranny in the hands of ideologically constituted majority, and the rule of law was changing into judicial arbitrariness.

Thus the youngster's mind, which in its previous embodiment had flirted with communism, can now, without any resistance, transfer its affection to liberal democracy, finding in it a source of similar ecstasy but reassurance that this system had never resorted and never would resort to the drastic measures known from the history of communism. Confident in the humanistic values of his new liberal-democratic creed, he infuses the old political institutions with new energy and injects them with new ideological content while remaining notoriously unaware that under new circumstances, these institutions are no longer what they once were and that they serve a new purpose.

A third narrative remains regarding the transition to the new system: the one about mankind's reaching and developing its full creative potential. Although once strongly emphasized, this eventually lost its importance and virtually disappeared. Regardless of the fact that some socialist visionaries tried to revive it from time to time, it had no place in communist reality. The new regime fell into the trap of gigantic practical problems. Who and for what purpose would consider humanity's achieving self-knowledge at a time when the people were desperately grappling with chronic scarcity and their leaders were courageously struggling with the new problems they themselves had created?

It is paradoxical that socialism, which began with a great humanistic message, not only quickly lowered its aspirations, but made them indistinguishable from the objectives that had already been realized—with much more success—by its main competitor, capitalism. The young Marx still used the language of Hegel to describe mankind's road to full flourishing, but the mature Marx chose to write about "surplus value," which clearly referred to economic exploitation and the way to overcome it. It is therefore hardly surprising that from the very beginning, the communist countries focused on the problem of labor, which, liberated from exploitation and the burden of "surplus value," would bring an unprecedented increase in productivity. These countries and their governments fought a never-ending but unfortunately persistently unsuccessful battle to produce enough goods for their citizens, and the more they failed, the more they aspired to superiority over capitalist economies. No matter how much they mobilized mass production, called for extra effort, designed ever more-ambitious five-year plans, the shortages of goods persisted, and the distance between the standard of living under capitalism and socialism steadily increased. No major economic problem was ever solved. All the riots and revolutions that broke out in communist countries had economic roots. This was not the only reason they occurred, but was nevertheless very important.

The communists also sought to provide citizens with adequate servings of pleasure to be enjoyed privately, but also, and more importantly, with their satisfaction showing for the world to see. At the beginning, the latter was confined to simple signs, usually by working men and women who, after a day's hard work, danced and sang in the streets to the tune of propagandistic songs. Over time, with progressive stabilization, the communists discovered that pleasure and entertainment were an extremely serious political matter. They realized that if a communist society was to resist the capitalist temptation, it should secure a comparable level of consumer goods for its citizens.

A model communist man was thus defined by three elements: ideology, work, and leisure. Once these three objectives were fulfilled, it was to be expected that the communist citizen would internalize his deep commitment to the system, work efficiently, and abandon for good the idea of the revolt, because after work he would have sufficient access to enjoyable activities. When compared to the full pathos of the declarations of the classics of Marxism promising man's spectacular flourishing under the communist system, it is hard indeed not to marvel about a dramatic reduction in expectations.

Liberal and democratic thought had been, from the very beginning—with few exceptions—minimalist when it came to its image of the human being. The triumph of liberalism and democracy was supposed to be emancipatory also in the sense that man was to become free from excessive demands imposed on him by unrealistic metaphysics invented by an aristocratic culture in antiquity and the Middle Ages. In other words, an important part of the message of modernity was to legitimize a lowering of human aspirations. Aspiring to great goals was not ruled out in particular cases, but greatness was no longer inscribed in the essence of humanity. The main principle behind the minimalist perspective was equality: from the point of view of a liberal order one cannot prioritize human objectives. Only the means can be prioritized in terms of efficiency, provided this does not jeopardize the rules of peaceful cooperation. ("It is neither less nor more rational to desire the wealth of Croesus than the poverty of a Buddhist monk," wrote the liberal economist Ludwig von Mises.)

There were, as I have said, exceptions to this view—few, but worth noting. Among the eighteenth-century authors, Kant, who defended liberalism, set up high standards for humanity; in the nineteenth century, John Stuart Mill and T. H. Green had similar intentions. The last two aptly perceived the danger of mediocrity that the democratic rule was inconspicuously imposing on modern societies. They both believed—differences notwithstanding—that some form of liberalism, or rather, a philosophy of liberty, was a possible remedy to the creeping disease of mediocrity. Mill remained under the partial, albeit indirect influence of German Romanticism, and thus attributed a particular role to great, creative individuals whose exceptionality or even eccentricity could—in a free environment—pull men out of a democratic slumber.

But these ideas did not find followers, and liberal-democratic thought and practice increasingly fell into the logic of minimalism. Lowering the requirements is a process that has no end. Once people become used to disqualifying certain standards as too high, impractical, or unnecessary, it is only a matter of time before natural inertia takes its course and even the new lowered standards are deemed unacceptable. One can look at the history of liberal democracy as a gradual sliding down from the high to the low, from the refined to the coarse. Quite often a step down has been welcomed as refreshing, natural, and healthy, and indeed it sometimes was. But whatever the merits of this process of simplification, it too often brought vulgarity to language, behavior, education, and moral rules. The growing vulgarity of form was particularly striking, especially in the last decades, moving away from sophistication and decorum. A liberal-democratic man refused to learn these artificial and awkward arrangements, the usefulness of which seemed to him at first doubtful, and soon—null. He felt he had no time for them, apparently believing that their absence would make life easier and more enjoyable. In their place he established new criteria: ease, practicality, usefulness, pleasure, convenience, and immediate gratification, the combination of which turned out to be a deadly weapon against the old social forms. The old customs crumbled, and so did rules of propriety, a sense of decorum, a respect for hierarchy.

These changes were often attributed to the deplorable influence of the bourgeoisie, the class that was said to embody the disappearance of forms and the vulgarity of the modern era. There was an immense output of creative works depicting the shallowness of the mercantile civilization. The antidote to commerce was—as evidenced by Thomas Mann's *Buddenbrooks* and John Galsworthy's *The Forsyte Saga*—art as a pure, disinterested expression of imagination in pursuit of the beautiful and the sublime. But over time it became clear that commerce and capitalism had been blamed somewhat hastily, and that the causes lay deeper. More perceptive thinkers soon realized that the very success of technology, productivity, and industry, that great achievement of the genius of modern man, was conducive, as José Ortega y Gasset persuasively argued, to the sterility of imagination and the triumph of self-satisfied pettiness. There was and still is something paradoxical in the fact that the historically unprecedented explosion of technology and industry, which brought wealth and security to millions of people and which would not have been possible without a high degree of creativity, was a major factor in reducing people's aspirations and, astonishingly, giving mediocrity a touch of respectability.

Man, feeling secure and enjoying the increasingly abundant benefits of a modern civilization, was slowly releasing himself from the compelling pressure of strict and demanding rules derived from religion and classical ethics. He was no longer in the mood to embark on a painful and uncertain journey to higher goals, on which John Stuart Mill elaborated with such hope. And his hopes were high. In a famous passage of his

Utilitarianism, he said that although man aspires to satisfy his drive for pleasure, he will always prefer to be an unsatisfied Socrates rather than a satisfied pig. Why? The argument was the following: man is cognizant of both states—the Socratic and the swinish—and there is no way that reason and conscience will allow him to opt for being a pig. The argument thus assumes in a unequivocal way that some ways of life are objectively better than others, that the Socratic model is clearly superior to that of a common man, and that there is nothing in human nature that can make people oblivious to this fact.

This last assumption, however, has been challenged since the very beginning of modern times. In liberal democracy, especially in recent decades, a generally acknowledged moral directive forbids looking down on people's moral priorities, because in the present society equality is the norm, not the hierarchy. But equality, as always, has its limitations. Mediocrity has been generally, though tacitly acknowledged as a non-controversial, if not preferred model, whereas the Socratic model, though nominally viewed as equal among others, has lost its appeal and support from the democratic mainstream as too aristocratic and elitist. In theory the Socratic way is as good as any other; in practice, it is hopelessly at odds with modern preferences. From a new perspective, the pig would seem, on reflection, a stronger competitor.

The gradual process in which the higher aspirations were being replaced by the lower tells us, no doubt, something about human nature: namely, that unless met with strong resistance or an attractive inspiration it shows a powerful tendency to be lured by the common and the mediocre. "Common," indeed, has ceased to be a word of disapproval in a liberal-democratic rhetoric, or rather, has ceased to be used at all. When so much is common, nothing really is. This change is but a small signal of a corruption of basic categories by which for centuries people described and evaluated their conduct.

Especially striking is a change in the meaning of the word "dignity," which since antiquity has been used as a term of obligation. If one was presumed to have dignity, one was expected to behave in a proper way as required by his elevated status. Dignity was something to be earned, deserved, and confirmed by acting in accordance with the higher standards imposed by a community or religion—for instance, by empowering a certain person with higher responsibilities or by claiming that man was created in God's image. Dignity was an attribute that ennobled those who acquired it. As noblesse oblige, dignity was an obligation to seek some form of self-improvement, however vaguely understood, but certainly closer to the Socratic way and further away from its opposite. The attribute was not bestowed forever: one could always lose it when acting in an undignified way.

At some point, the concept of dignity was given a different meaning, contrary to the original. This happened mainly through the intercession of the language of human rights, especially after the 1948 Universal Declaration. The idea of human beings having inalienable rights is counterintuitive and extremely difficult to justify. It may make some philosophical sense if derived from a strong theory of human nature such as one finds in classical metaphysics. However, when we accept a weak theory, attributing to human beings only elementary qualities, and deliberately disregarding strong metaphysical assumptions, then the idea of rights loses its plausibility. It may, of course, be sanctioned as a mere product of legislation through a Parliamentary or court ruling, which entitles people to make various claims called "rights," but these claims will be no more than arbitrary decisions by particular groups of politicians or judges who choose to do this rather than that due to circumstances, ideology, or individual predilections or under pressure from interest groups. It would indeed be silly to call such claims "inalienable," because inalienability by definition cannot be legislated.

Thus, in order to strengthen the unjustified and, within the accepted conceptual framework, unjustifiable notion of human rights, the concept of dignity was invoked, but in a peculiar way so as to make it seem to imply more than it actually did. This concept created an illusion of a strong view of human nature, and of endowing this nature with qualities nowhere explicitly specified but implying something noble, being an immortal soul, an innate desire for good, etc. But on the other hand, in using this concept, unaccompanied by other qualifications, the framers of the human rights documents apparently felt exempted from any need to present an explicit and serious philosophical interpretation of human nature and to explain the grounds and the conditions on which one could conceive of its dignity. This operation—or more precisely, sleight of hand, and not very fair to boot—led to a sudden revival of the concept of human dignity, but with a radically different meaning.

Since the issue of the Universal Declaration dignity has no longer been about obligation, but about claims and entitlements. The new dignity did not oblige people to strive for any moral merits or deserts; it allowed them to submit whatever claims they wished, and to justify these claims by referring to a dignity that they possessed by the mere fact of being born without any moral achievement or effort. A person who desired to achieve the satisfaction of a pig was thus equally entitled to appeal to dignity to justify his goals as another who tried to follow the path of Socrates, and each time, for a pig and for a Socrates, this was the same dignity. A right to be a pig and a right to be a Socrates were, in fact, equal and stemmed from the same moral (or rather nonmoral, as the new dignity practically broke off with morality) source.

Having armed himself with rights, modern man found himself in a most comfortable situation with no precedent: he no longer had to justify his claims and actions as long as he qualified them as rights. Regardless of what demands he would make on the basis of those rights and for what purpose he would use them, he did not and, in fact, could not lose his dignity, which he had acquired for life simply by being born human. And since having this dignity carried no obligation to do anything particularly good or worthy, he could, while constantly invoking it, make claims that were increasingly more absurd and demand justification for ever more questionable activities. Sinking more and more into arrogant vulgarity, he could argue that this vulgarity not only did not contradict his inborn dignity, but it could even, by a stretch of the imagination, be treated as some sort of an achievement. After all, can a dignity that is inborn and constitutes the essence of humanness, generate anything that would be essentially undignified and nonhuman? The dignity-based notion of human rights was thus both a powerful factor to legitimize a minimalist concept of human nature, and its legitimate child. Moreover, it equipped modern anthropological minimalism with the instruments of self-perpetuation, the most efficient instruments of this kind ever devised in the history of the Western societies.

★ 6 ★

Work and entertainment (plus, as we shall see later, ideology) that shaped a human existence in communism and gave basic content to people's lives more or less reflected, but also caricatured, what was happening to modern man in the capitalist civilization.

In modern times, work became something more than earning means for survival and material security; it was a vocation, which gave human life discipline, meaning, and order. If we are to believe Max Weber, the first stirrings of this epoch-making change had a religious character. His argument was the following. The initiating factor was an acute and unbearable awareness—typical of early Protestantism—of the sinfulness of human nature. This turned men's minds to work, which they began to treat as an expression of piety imposing on human sinfulness some form of discipline. But because the fruits of work could not be enjoyed—such enjoyment would be sinful—one could not consume them. And because they could not be consumed, then—and this is where the actual civilizational revolution happened—they had to be invested.

This was a fundamental change. What it meant was that, for the first time on such a scale in their history, people abandoned a deeply embedded desire to seek wealth simply as a means to indulge in expensive and extravagant whims. Work still produced wealth, as it was always hoped it would, but was no longer valued primarily as a means to consumption. Disciplined work became its own proper reward, devoid of dreams about future joys and satisfied temptations, being completely rationalized and subordinated to a long-term plan of action. In Weber's view, this new approach to consumption—as being separated from pleasure and postponed to an indefinite future—was at the root of an unprecedented economic growth that was brought about by capitalism.

Weber's analyses give us a good insight into why and how modern thinking justified the lowering of aspirations. A minimalistic view of human nature, initially apparent first and foremost in Protestantism but later on expanding to other areas of the Western world, had a specific nature. The basic cause of the change was purely religious: a new doctrine of predestination as well as a fundamental weight attributed to the original sin precluded any form of moral and spiritual perfectibility. Big plans for man were no longer feasible. But at the same time, the low level to which human aspirations were reduced acquired a noble, sometimes even heroic trait, which—let us add—completely disappeared together with the liberalization of the Protestant doctrine. It is true that man acknowledged his powerlessness vis-à-vis the great plans—those plans that in the past were said to lead him into vanity—but he put all his energy and will into doing as best as he could in the lower realm, the only one accessible to him because of his corrupted nature, and this realm was work.

This paradoxical view of human nature brought about by the Protestant revolution—man belittled his status, while at the same time drastically increasing his requirements within the lower realm—could not for too long retain its viability. The natural downward pull of minimalism turned out to be stronger, as the initial discipline had to become less and less compelling. At some point, the old capitalism, which had rejected consumerism and owed its success precisely to this rejection, was transformed into a system in which consumption not only came to be accepted, but in fact took control of the entire economic mechanism, and gradually marginalized most human incentives, eventually to become the single most powerful source of motivation. The road to this stage was complex and getting there took a long time, but before this happened, the modern bourgeois civilization had its long period of glory when, by having espoused the classic concept of human nature and releasing all channels of human creativity through the capitalist revolution, it managed to transform spectacularly our civilization and to accomplish extraordinary things in all areas of life.

The consumerist change was of course to be expected by some and welcomed by many. Mr. Gradgrind of Dickens's *Hard Times*—a strict, fanatically disciplined modern man, mercilessly attempting to eradicate human weaknesses—is a despicable figure and as such perfectly illustrates a negative perception of a classical capitalist by the humanist critics of a modern society. Mr. Gradgrind is deaf to temptations, unresponsive to warm emotions and simple pleasures, motivated purely by new rationality and by nothing else. His callousness seems almost inhuman. But capitalism finally changed, and the severity of the world's Gradgrinds disappeared. The religious background of the new economy so persuasively described by Weber evaporated, and the capitalism itself—while continuing the ethic of the discipline of work and pushing productivity to new records of efficiency and inventiveness—liberated itself completely from the Protestant gloom.

The liberal-democratic society abandoned the old time rigor without regret. The discipline of work and high requirements of productivity persisted in the new times, but in other matters man refused to go back to his previous self. Once having made a decision about having his aspirations reduced, he unabashedly enjoined the new situation and compensated the strict work imperatives by his ever-increasing indulgence in entertainment. But this new predilection, so different from his previous somberness, had consequences unanticipated and even unfathomed by Weber. Naturally, entertainment always constituted a strong inclination of human existence, but for centuries it was rigorously separated from the serious component of man's life. Lent and Carnival could not be confused because each of them responded to different needs and performed different functions. But when the minimalistic anthropology took hold, the barriers separating one from the other weakened and the temptation to give entertainment more and more prominence became irresistible, particularly in societies in which the fear of sin had lost its deterring power.

In today's world entertainment is not just a pastime or a style, but a substance that permeates everything: schools and universities, upbringing of children, intellectual life, art, morality, and religion. It has become dear to the hearts of students, professors, entrepreneurs, journalists, engineers, scientists, writers, even priests. Entertainment imposes itself psychologically, intellectually, socially, and also, strange as it might sound, spiritually. A failure to provide human endeavors—even the most noble ones—with an entertaining wrapping is today unthinkable and borders on sin.

The modern sense of entertainment increasingly resembles what Pascal long ago called divertissement: that is, an activity—as he wrote in his *Thoughts*—that separates us from the seriousness of existence and fills this existence with false content. Divertissement is thus not only being entertained in the ordinary sense of the word, but living and acting within artificial rules that organize our lives, setting conventional and mostly trivial goals which we pursue, getting involved in disputes and competitions, aspiring to honors-making careers, and doing everything that would turn our thoughts away from fundamental existential matters. By escaping the questions of the ultimate meaning of our own lives, or of human life in general, our minds slowly get used to that fictitious reality, which we take for the real one, and are lured by its attractions.

The difference between Pascal's divertissement and today's entertainment—or, rather, having fun, as it has become customary to say—is that the modern man, no matter how much a desire to have fun has captured his soul, knows very well that it is an artificial construction, not the real thing. Whether some other, more objective reality exists is to him a matter of indifference, and if told there is not, he would probably still remained unmoved. Having neutralized all musings about objectivity, the modern man takes pride in his deep involvement in entertainment, which in the absence of other objective references he considers natural.

This aspect of entertainment and the disturbing consequences of its present reign came under scrutiny nearly a century ago; since then its absorbing presence and its impact on human life have increased immeasurably. It is interesting that both the conservatives defending the classic view of human nature and some of the socialists of the Frankfurt School, while having fundamental disagreements, described this new phenomenon in similar terms, and were equally alarmed by the extent to which the human mind was degraded and enslaved by what was claimed to be an extremely pleasant, unproblematic, but somehow superior form of freedom. Both groups feared that the hegemony and omnipresence of entertainment might effectively dilute a sense of the seriousness of existence as well as the type of mindset that gives this seriousness a proper role in thought and action. For the first time in the entire history of mankind there appeared a type of human being who thought that not having been surrounded by entertainment from cradle to grave in all areas of life was an anomaly.

Of course, liberal democracy should not be singled out as the only cause of this mental revolution. There were other causes: capitalism, secularism, technology, and other equally important factors. The fact is, however, that for important reasons liberal democracy and entertainment found enthusiastic allies in each other. Entertainment became the most obvious and direct manifestation of freedom that liberalism offered humanity and, at the same time, the most tangible confirmation of the dominant status of the democratic man and his tastes. To be sure, his dominance was larger, deeper, and more consequential and by no means exhausted itself in an inner necessity to have fun. And yet the omnipresence of entertainment was something by which the democratic man became easily recognized: it was his trademark, his coat of arms, his—so to speak—symbolic identity card.

Once we assume anthropological minimalism to be a key to understanding today's liberal democracy, it becomes clear why the liberal democrats wholeheartedly embraced a belief in the inevitability of history. This belief was, of course, a legitimate offspring of the Enlightenment faith in progress, to which the liberal democrats are even more committed than the socialists, themselves also partly the disciples of the Enlightenment dogmas. In view of the fact that the liberal-democratic civilization brought a spectacular development of technology and succeeded in providing millions of people with the benefits of modernity, the belief in the inexorability of progress is—at least within the limits delineated by the liberal-democratic mind—not without rational foundations.

The primary source of the belief in unidirectional history is thus man himself. A remarkable correlation exists between the regime and the man, one that had never in history been achieved on a similar scale. The communists attempted to mold a communist man to fit the institution and logic of the communist system, but suffered defeat. But where they failed, the liberal democrats proved successful. If ever any system existed that was perfectly tailored to the aspirations of the people inhabiting it, it was liberal democracy, and if ever any human model existed that was perfectly tailored to opportunities offered by the political system and to the aspirations enhanced by it, it was a liberal-democratic man.

Alternative political models have not been drawn or even seriously considered, and the effectiveness of the regime is still impressively high. Therefore, an expansion of liberal democracy will probably continue, and the system will continue to confirm the set of beliefs that the inhabitant of the regime not only claims to live by, but also holds to be the only set of beliefs that are worth living by. He feels privileged and lucky not to be like those unfortunate fools or rascals who have failed to accept the obvious. All these factors taken together reinforce his belief that if the world is to survive and develop, it must move in one and only one direction—his own.

This view has become contagious, and it quickly spread to the communist countries at the time when they faced fundamental future choices after having parted with the old regime. One would think that the fall of an unpopular, coercive, and evil regime would provide a unique opportunity for the nation to develop its own institutions at every level of social and political life, the institutions that would be responsive to its own needs, bearing witness to its own historical experience, and reinforcing a sense of a newly gained freedom and autonomy. This was the time when the creative potential of the nation, released from a long period of enslavement, should have manifested itself most fully and most enthusiastically. But in Eastern Europe this was not the case. As if charmed by powerful but invisible political magicians, the East Europeans immediately succumbed to what they considered to be the imperative of the historical development of Western civilization. The required attitude of a newly liberated nation was not that of creativity, but conformity.

The events that took place after 1989 shattered the illusions many people harbored, which in the recent past had not seemed illusions at all, but had possessed some degree of credibility. Poland may be a case in point. Everything indicated that dramatic and painful historical experience should make the Poles particularly suspicious of the new grandiose political projects aiming at restructuring the entire social substance. The riots that erupted more or less once per decade since 1945, when the Soviet Union imposed a communist system on Polish society, were read as an expression of such suspicions.

There is no better illustration of this desire than the period of the so-called first Solidarity in 1980–1981. In July and August of 1980, workers held massive strikes against lawlessness and economic chaos, which led to the establishment of a powerful trade union in Poland, the first such big independent organization in the Soviet bloc. But the first Solidarity was not just a trade union, and the demands it raised were not simply about the fair distribution of wealth, increases in wages and benefits, and workers' guarantees. The union's program also included more general demands, far exceeding those ordinary human aspirations that seem all but natural in a permanently inefficient economy with humiliatingly low wages and notorious shortages of goods. Solidarity stood up in defense of human dignity (in its original and not the corrupted sense), access to culture, respect for truth in science and for nobility in art, and a proper role given to Christian heritage and Christian religion. It seemed that suddenly those great ideas at the root of Western civilization—which this civilization had slowly begun to forget—were again brought to life and ignited like a fire in the minds of the members of a trade union. This was probably one of the reasons why Solidarity met with such widespread, though short-lived admiration. Suddenly, in this godforsaken place there emerged a movement that not only challenged the Evil Empire, but reminded everyone of the spiritual dimension of human existence, of truth, God, heroism, nobility of culture, the importance of historical and religious heritage, and other high moral principles.

During the period of the second Solidarity, in 1988–1989, the final chapter of the communist rule in Poland, this mood disappeared almost without a trace, and although the possibility of political victory was nearer than ever, the big ideas and ambitious plans lost their appeal. This change of attitude was somewhat understandable, considering the pressure of circumstances and, after the communists lost their monopoly, an urgent need to resolve vast numbers of practical problems. But the fact remains that the new Poland, like other countries in the region, quickly discarded the higher concerns expressed by the first Solidarity and almost immediately adopted a minimalist perspective in order to conform to the atmosphere and practice of western liberal democracy. Once big ideas were gone, work and entertainment seized the imagination of the people and turned them into copies of a standard liberal-democratic model.

Poland shook off the communist yoke at a time when the Western world had already reached a phase of considerable homogeneity and standardization. Therefore as soon as the Poles liberated themselves and started aspiring to the liberal-democratic world, Poland lost its previous exotic charm as a country in which workers, intellectuals, and priests defied communism, prayed to God, and risked their freedom in defense of truth, good, and beauty. The liberal-democratic world did not want such exoticism in their midst, and would have been embarrassed if the Poles had persisted in their initial ambitions. It expected a different Poland, the one that was indistinguishable from other nations, following this or that pattern of liberal-democratic order, provided it covered all areas of social life. The Poles grasped this quickly and the majority of them adapted to the expectations without protest and without regret. There was, of course, an unpleasant side to it. The societies that liberated themselves from the old rules adopted new ones, but were unaware that the new rules gave them less liberty and fewer opportunities than they had naïvely hoped, being blinded by the radiant vision of the free world.

Many East Europeans were ready to admit that, although the world was not moving inexorably toward communism—as the Communists had tried to convince them for a long time and with relatively good results—it still moved inevitably in another direction. Just as the Soviet Union had been the vanguard of progress before, so now it was "the West," which often meant the United States and sometimes the European Union. The East Europeans were supposed to follow in their footsteps. The metaphors of catching up and a race were often used to describe the situation of the societies that joined the world of liberal democracy: "they" were somewhere in front of "us," rushing fast forward, while we remained in the back, trying to make up for lost time by doing all the things that they did, but in a shorter period of time. The result was that innovation and inventiveness—so much talked about, praised, and encouraged by all and sundry, and paid homage to in words—could not be taken seriously as challenges, and never became a really respected attitude: the deeper wisdom was to copy and to imitate. The more we copied and imitated, the more we were glad of ourselves. Institutions, education, customs, law, media, language, almost everything became all of a sudden imperfect copies of the originals that were in the line of progress ahead of us.

CHAPTER II

Utopia

Communism and liberal democracy are believed to be the ultimate stages of the history of political transformations. The Marxists contended that communism was the last act of human drama and that, once it was achieved, there was no incentive or reason to strive for anything superior. Similarly, according to its followers nothing politically superior can arise in the wake of liberal democracy, which, per a common though rarely explicitly articulated conviction, exhausted the process of political transformations. If there is such a thing as an ability to hypothesize possible political arrangements, this cannot lead us, in the first case, beyond communism, or in the second, beyond liberal democracy.

Both communism and liberal democracy are therefore perceived— from an inside perspective—as having no alternatives. The only change that one could imagine happening was one for the worse, which in the eyes of supporters meant not a slight deterioration, but a disaster. The communist would say: if communism is rejected or prevented, then society will continue to be subjected to class exploitation, capitalism, imperialism, and fascism. The liberal democrats would say: if liberal democracy is not accepted, then society will fall prey to authoritarianism, fascism, and theocracy. In both cases, the search for an alternative solution is, at best, nonsensical and not worth a moment's reflection, and at worst, a highly reckless and irresponsible game.

The belief that socialism had no alternatives stemmed from a presupposition that this system eliminated the root causes of social and economic conflicts, which—it will be recalled—allegedly set in motion the machine that in the course of history transformed one political order into another. By fully implementing the idea of class justice, communism put an end, once and for all, to that state of disequilibrium from which societies suffered since the earliest stages of their existence. Attacking the socialist order was therefore not a normal political activity, but a monstrous sin, an assault on the most precious achievement in the entire history of humanity.

Liberal democracy is also viewed by its supporters as the final realization of the eternal desires of mankind, particularly those of freedom and the rule of the people. If—as did the liberals—we interpret history as a complex set of conflicts that slowly but irresistibly maximized the freedom of the individual and—as did the democrats—as a comparably complex set of conflicts that slowly, but irresistibly liberated the people from tyranny and empowered them with political instruments of self-government, then liberal democracy will indeed seem to be a happy ending of the eternal human dreams. Because it is extremely difficult to imagine something that might follow this last stage of historical development without constituting an improved version of it, it is equally difficult to imagine that anyone who is morally balanced and of a sound mind could in good faith act against liberal democracy and the ideals it embodied.

It is therefore more than natural that both systems identified existing structures with human ideals. Communism was social justice, and social justice was communism. This marriage between the system and the ideal gave birth to a peculiar type of mentality, inadvertently prone to political moralizing. Living in such a system one could not simply describe facts or express one's political persuasion because everything had to be entangled in the phraseology referring to the good of humanity, the liberation of peoples, the wickedness of imperialism, the blessings of a classless society, and the happiness of life under socialism. From the very beginning, socialism/communism was sanctioned in moralistic terms without which it was as a system inconceivable; every communist or socialist, even if cynical and cruel, was compelled to see some communist and socialist ideals reflected even in the simplest matters and could not express the simplest thought without referring to them.

Liberal democracy boasts of bestowing freedom on individuals and emancipation on groups, while simultaneously taking it for granted that freedom and emancipation are possible only in a liberal democracy, or rather, that freedom and emancipation *are* liberal democracy. Over time, the mind of a liberal democrat began to resemble that of a socialist, exhibiting the same tendency to combine the languages of morality and politics, as no other discourse could possibly do justice to the nature of the system. There are no topics, no matter how trivial, that the liberal democrat could raise or discuss without mentioning freedom, discrimination, equality, human rights, emancipation, authoritarianism, and other related notions. No other language is used or even accepted.

Both assertions about the unity of institutions and ideals—those of the communists and the liberal democrats—are completely unfounded. Communism did not represent class justice, nor was liberal democracy the sole representative of freedom. In the case of communism the truth may seem little controversial today given that the crimes committed under its slogans exceed human imagination.

The portrayal of liberal democracy as a realization of the eternal desire for freedom is very popular, almost verging on a platitude, especially in recent decades. This picture is false. First, liberalism was certainly not the only orientation expressing the desire for freedom, nor was it particularly consistent in this devotion. The supporters of republicanism, conservatism, romanticism, Christianity, and many other movements also demanded freedom, and did a lot to advance its cause. If freedom as we understand it in Western civilization is not only an abstract value, but has a concrete shape well-grounded in institutions, social practices, and mental habits, then the contribution of liberalism is one of many, far from decisive. It is hard to imagine freedom without classical philosophy and the heritage of antiquity, without Christianity and scholasticism, without different traditions in the philosophy of law and political and social practices, without ancient and modern republicanism, without strong anthropology and ethics of virtues and duties, without Anglo-Saxon and continental conservatism or many other components of the entire Western civilization.

Liberal democrats circumvent this objection in such a way that they attribute the term "liberal" to everything they think succeeded in making a breakthrough in the walls of oppression and authority. This allows them to accept that Socrates was a "liberal" compared to Plato; the Sophists were liberals compared to Socrates; Ockham compared to St. Thomas; Erasmus compared to Luther; Luther compared to Calvin, and so on. In this somewhat bizarre view, liberalism—whether democratic or not yet democratic—existed in Western culture from the very beginning but only in the modern day did it gain momentum and finally triumph in recent times. Such lavish squandering of the term "liberal" is obviously fraudulent and constitutes a completely unjustified attempt to elevate liberalism to a privileged position, allowing it to grant favors to some and taking them away from others.

When we look at the activities of liberals in the course the last hundred years, it turns out that they were quite dogmatic on the issue of freedom on a theoretical level, but very opportunistic in practice. They did not shun seeking allies in enlightened absolutisms. In the twentieth century they engaged in a long-term flirtation with socialism, including its Soviet version, being probably motivated by a similar assumption. Even the most liberal of liberals displayed extraordinary softness against the Soviet Union and the Soviet communism and sometimes even actively supported the idea of unilateral disarmament of the West, as did libertarians—all in the name of freedom. Liberals also showed weakness against terrorism and the left-wing dictatorships in the Third World, but many of them reacted with noticeable self-restraint when it came to the anticommunist activities of groups in the Soviet bloc countries. Their freedom-related account is therefore not overly clean.

★ 2 ★

The above similarities point to something more significant. Both systems, by being final, meet the criteria by which we define utopianism. Both are—simply—utopias. A note of clarification is required, however. A widely accepted, though not accurate definition states that the word "utopia" denotes a political project that is idealistic in its intentions, but completely unrealistic, impractical, and incompatible with human experience. The creators of utopias are therefore usually looked down upon as naïve senti-mentalists or feared as dangerously inhuman social engineers.

This definition is wrong. None of the great utopians created their blueprints for a good society with the assumption that those plans were completely devoid of practical value. None of them considered himself to be a dreamer, deliberately separating himself from and ignoring all lessons of human experience. What indeed would have been the point of such fantasies? Who would have devoted the time and energy to create political projects that were politically useless? The designers of utopias knew very well, and often admitted that, given the circumstances, the implementation of their projects would be difficult, extremely difficult, or even unlikely. Yet they never had the slightest doubt about their func-tional value and their intention was to put them to practice.

Utopia is thus not a political fantasy but a bold project, bolder than others because it aims at a solution to all the basic problems of collective life that humanity has faced since it began to organize itself politically. Utopia is—I beg the reader's pardon for such a vile-sounding phrase—the final solution. Following its implementation, injustice, poverty, tyranny, and other political sins will disappear once and for all. Their disappear-ance will be structural and not depend on contingent factors.

The first utopias were written about in the Renaissance, the period when belief in human greatness was a primary article of faith as well a major intellectual and artistic incentive. The message was simple—man can achieve greatness and be equal to God, because he has an unlimited creative potential. Yes, he can fall lower than the beasts, but he can also reach higher than ever before, as there is no upper limit to knowledge or art. The greatness thesis led to another argument in the centuries that followed. While it was true that great artists created extraordinary works of painting, music, and literature, and also superb works in mathematics, philosophy, and physics, it was equally true that in one area human genius had not yet appeared—politics. Why not, then, create a great political work of art? Why not devise a political construction that would be com-parable to other great human achievements? Utopia was precisely to be such a political masterpiece. To put it differently: the human race gave the world Dante, Plato, and Aeschylus, and later still Bach, Shakespeare, and other geniuses, and it was now high time that it had its genius of political creation. The fact that so far no political masterpiece had been created did not mean that creativity in politics was an exception to human greatness, but that the attempts were not sufficiently vigorous or that such a great political artist had not yet been born.

Communism was to be such a masterpiece. It is true that Karl Marx viewed utopias with contempt, attributing the term "utopian" to his socialist opponents, invariably with an attitude of annoyance. He used this word in a colloquial sense, however, which gave him grounds to accuse previous generations of socialists of a faulty reading of reality. They naïvely believed—in fact they did not, but this is what he said—that socialism would triumph simply by its own intrinsic righteousness. And this belief he angrily rejected: the mere attractiveness of a political ideal did not make it practically feasible. The world—he said—was not malleable to human whims, and any change must derive from an accurate description of the objective laws according to which the world develops.

After these rather simple-minded criticisms he felt entitled to refer to his own theory as "scientific," which was later repeated with delight by his followers, from Engels and Lenin through Stalin and to the teachers of Marxism in the Soviet bloc countries. The scientific nature of socialism, however, had been dubious from the start because it was not clear what science was behind it and what it was supposed to justify. Such a science, of course, did not exist. The most that can be said was that socialism was backed by some sort of theory of society and history, which in no case was scientific. Its justification of socialism as a political structure did not even meet the criteria of a decent argument. Thus, serious scholars of Marx's socialism—such as Leszek Kołakowski—had no doubt that it was a utopia. It was the movement's utopian and not scientific nature that made the Marxist version of communism so phenomenally popular.

The utopianism of liberal democracy is not so obvious. Besides, liberalism and democracy are not related to utopian thinking in the same way. Initially, liberalism, especially in some economic versions, seemed anti-utopian because it precluded any perfect and ultimate form of economic order. Free-market economy was even called "the dismal science" to emphasize the gloomy aspect of its consequences. But there were also highly optimistic versions according to which the free market was a miraculous instrument to eliminate war and bring about the global brotherhood of humanity in a future era of commerce. Commerce, it will be recalled, was seen as the trademark of the new civilization of peace, wealth, and stability.

This rediscovery of liberal utopianism in the twentieth century, especially in free-market theories, can be easily explained. It is enough to imagine a liberal order in its simplicity—free-market without any state intervention, and individual rights unregulated by the state except the general rules of cooperation—and to realize that these simple mechanisms have never really been tried. For some liberals such simplicity will be tempting, precisely because the liberal solution has never been applied in undiluted form; there were always compromises with other political and economic systems, with traditionally inherited institutions, or with people's conservatism. But once we do away with the mitigating factors and try the free-market solution uncompromisingly and radically, we will have a pure system, a splendidly simple and universally applicable mechanism to solve all major problems. In short, we will have a utopia.

The utopian tendency had yet an extra dimension. Economic liberals could not get over the popularity of socialism, which they considered a completely irrational idea, but which for reasons with which they were never satisfied managed to touch the hearts and minds of millions of people throughout the world. This tremendous success of their main enemy made them critically reassess the previous methods by which the free marketers wanted to win popular support. The failure of the free market in the contest of popularity, they thought, was precisely that—contrary to socialism—it never existed in its simple and pure form, and that this never happened because of the weakness and half-heartedness of its message. And so they concluded: if the free market is presented not in a timid, apologetic, and cowardly way, but in proud openness as an optimal answer to every important problem, if it officially, as it were, entered into an ideological race with socialism as a superior all-encompassing formula, it must and would win. Once the economic liberals drew this conclusion, they deliberately and consciously started using the term "utopia" for what they were advocating. After all, what can be more attractive than a utopia that works? And work it must—they said.

Some liberals could not even conceal their bewilderment that such a fantastic project as theirs, giving everyone, literally everyone, the freedom to pursue their own desires, had not yet caught human imagination strongly enough. So they openly spoke of a liberal utopia to promote what they thought to be the only one worth the name. Friedrich von Hayek, Ludwig von Mises, Ayn Rand, Robert Nozick, and many other libertarians did precisely this. It went far beyond the realm of the free market. As Nozick wrote in his famous work under the symptomatic title *Anarchy, State, and Utopia*, what the liberals advocated was not just another utopia, but rather a utopia of utopias, or in other words, a regime that would include all other regimes, a final order incorporating all other orders. With this, the millennia-long dispute about which system was supreme would be finally resolved. The utopia of utopias would offer a place for everyone to have and strive for his own concept of a utopia, for socialists and conservatives, royalists and egalitarians, and everyone else. The utopia of all utopias would be—as Nozick claimed—"the only morally legitimate state, the only morally tolerable one," the state "that best realizes the utopian aspirations of untold dreamers and visionaries." To call it a utopia of utopias was to give it "luster . . . to thrill the heart or inspire people to struggle or sacrifice . . . to man barricades under its banner."

Democracy did not have obvious links with utopian thinking. Since antiquity, democracy had been considered one of the defective systems; not better but certainly not worse than oligarchy or monarchy. Plato and Aristotle gave us an insightful critical analysis of it, taking as evidence the functioning of the democratic experience in ancient Athens. Much of what they said has a lot of validity today even though the ancient democracy differed considerably from what passes for a democratic regime today. Plato and Aristotle were not the only critics of the system. In fact, it is extremely difficult to find a classical philosopher who would be its defender. Democritus was one of the few; some scholars also mention Protagoras, although his democratic credentials are highly problematic.

The ancient philosophers' primary question was what makes the best regime. Democracy certainly did not qualify. Why not? The answer was simple. They thought democracy was a messy system, systematically undermining the rule of law, profoundly partisan, often hostile to the most prominent leaders and citizens. The famous defense of democratic Athens delivered by Pericles in Thucydides' *The Peloponnesian War* is in fact more a defense of Athens and Athenian imperialism than of the democratic political model. When Plato and Aristotle wrote their scathing remarks about the Athenian system, they thought it was already in decline and Athens might soon become a victim of the crisis from which it would not be able to recover. And this is exactly what happened.

In early modernity, this classical view of democracy did not change much. Political thinkers were interested in why and how the state comes about, how it should work, how to secure its stability, and who the sovereign is. In all these considerations, the problem of democracy was relegated to a secondary or even tertiary place; there was no challenge to the ancient theory that it was a defective system. When the Founding Fathers were creating the foundations of the American republic, they treated democracy—as well as other political models—with great suspicion and therefore devised a complex political mechanism to alleviate its weaknesses. When Tocqueville observed the same society a few decades later, however, he had no doubts about its democratic character. By then, democracy had not only driven out all political alternatives and become the sole ruler of the American mind, but revealed itself in such an imposing way that the democratic scenario seemed to the French aristocrat to be the destiny of all Western societies. Such a perspective did not make him happy and he finished his book on a clearly pessimistic note: democracy was more a problem than a solution. What he saw at the end of the democratic road was a new despotism, different from earlier despotic regimes, invisible but dangerously enslaving people's minds, accepted willingly by the demos as the most genuine representation of the people's desires.

Unconditional praise of democracy—absurd in the light of classical political theory—was for a long time first and foremost an American specialty. However, the global triumph of democracy—the liberal democracy, actually—had to wait a little longer. E. M. Forster is famous for saying that it deserved two cheers, not three, which is exactly as many as Irving Kristol granted to capitalism several decades later. In his famous aphorism, Churchill indirectly acknowledged the old truth that democracy was not a political masterpiece, though—and it was something new—he seemed to hint that it was superior to other regimes, which was tantamount to granting it a position it had never occupied before.

A few decades later all ambiguities were gone, and if the slogan "three cheers for democracy" came from nobody's pen, it was only because there were better compliments at hand. Democracy was spoken of—by Pierre Rosanvallon, among others—as an "unfinished project," that is, one that was constantly being revised, still undergoing improvements, never completed, and still allowing a lot of room for human creativity. It was democracy constantly democratizing itself so as to surpass democracy (or something equally vague, almost meaningless). Similar remarks about democratic democracy, or *démocratie à venir*, or democracy so democratic that it continues to go beyond democracy, were to be found in Derrida. Finally, the word "utopia" had to appear, and it did. The man who called the liberal-democratic political system a utopia was John Rawls, the greatest of the great authorities on all the supporters, advocates, and analysts of the system, and the maker of what might be called today's liberal-democratic orthodoxy. When he said it, no one was surprised. With his clear Anglo-Saxon mind, Rawls expressed in public what many had been thinking for some time, but did not dare to speak aloud.

★ 3 ★

Let us return for a moment to Churchill's famous quote. It comes from the speech that he delivered at the British House of Commons in 1947 and reads as follows: "Many forms of Government have been tried and will be tried in this world of sin and woe. No one pretends that democracy is perfect or all-wise. Indeed, it has been said that democracy is the worst form of government except all those other forms that have been tried from time to time."

This statement had a life of its own and was repeatedly twisted or modified according to the intentions of those invoking it. Two versions with two different interpretations stand out. The first one is a mild paradox: "Democracy is the worst political system, except for all the others." The sentence contains two main pieces of information about democracy's standing in a paradoxical relation to other systems: democracy is flawed (after all, it is the worst) and at the same time it is superior to other regimes (therefore, it turns out not to be the worst because the others are even worse). If we assume that the first piece of information is more important, then the lesson drawn from Churchill's statement would partly concur with what the ancients wrote about the power of the people: that it is a highly imperfect system, and therefore requires great vigilance and implementation of corrective mechanisms that may also be undemocratic. Churchill did not identify any particular fault of democracy, but one could read into it a suggestion of moderate skepticism and criticism of democratic procedures. But it was not that message of skepticism and criticism, however toned down, that won the hearts of millions of supporters of democracy around the world.

Another conclusion, different from the previous one, gained much larger support. The reasoning was simple: it was enough to treat the second piece of information as a basic one—that all other regimes are more defective—and to ignore completely the first part—that democracy also has many faults. This gave the conclusion an unambiguously pro-democratic meaning: not that democracy is the least objectionable of all regimes, but that it is the best one. And if it is the best, its defects are negligible. With this twist of meaning, any criticism of democracy becomes unfounded, and any critic irresponsible and not worth listening to: there is no sense in criticizing something that by definition is superior to the alternatives. The crowning step of this reasoning was that whatever democracy's shortcomings, they can be removed by more democracy; the best cannot be corrected by anything but the best.

When we take a look at each conclusion separately in the above reasoning, we can easily see that they in fact constitute a series of unsubstantiated claims. The sequence of the steps is as follows:

1. all systems other than democracy are worse than democracy;
2. democracy is the best political system;
3. democracy must not be criticized because such criticism may undermine something for which there is no better alternative;
4. only democracy is acceptable, and therefore all changes and adjustments in democracy can be performed by democratic means;
5. the remedy for the weaknesses of democracy is more democracy.

Each subsequent step was made by adding more content to the previous one, which resulted in a gradual departure from the initial statement, which created—finally—a huge chasm between propositions (i) and (v). Proposition (i) expressed a rather skeptical view about all regimes, including democracy, whose advantage over its rivals was its somewhat less-imperfect nature. Proposition (v) is an enthusiastic declaration of faith in democracy and absolute condemnation of everything undemocratic. Someone who asserted (i) cannot—without violating logic—smoothly pass to assert (v).

This last assertion's absurdity leaps to the eye, but in spite of that it is today regarded, surprisingly, as an expression of a profound political wisdom. To see this absurdity, no special insight is needed: an excess of anything is never good. After all, no one will claim that the shortcomings of oligarchy can be removed by extending oligarchy, flaws of tyranny by expanding tyranny, defects and disadvantages of monarchy by increasing the element of monarchy. Nobody in his right mind will claim that progressive monopolization is a cure for monopoly and that the remedy for anarchy is more anarchy. Why then, if we agree that democracy has its weaknesses, would such weaknesses be reduced by having more democracy? In what way will more democracy reduce, for example, democratic vulgarity, or the cult of mediocrity, or the weakening of social customs and traditions, or the overproduction of legislation, or the omnipresent spirit of partisanship penetrating every aspect of life? If the increasing role of the masses led to the vulgarization of culture, why would placing even greater importance on the same masses lead to culture's refinement? If democracy introduces yet further groups in the political and legislative process and provides them with the tools to secure their interests through legislation, which, in turn, leads to legislative excesses, then why would the increased number of these groups and their increased influence generate legislative restraint? And so forth, and so on.

Let us note that a similar rhetoric was used in communism. When faced with the notoriously recurring symptoms of the decay of the system, communist rulers and propagandists euphemistically called them "distortions," always saying that these resulted from the deviation from socialism and that more genuine socialism was needed to set things right. No empirical experience could support this claim—in fact the opposite seemed truer and truer every day—but evidence usually has little value against a strong political faith.

Both claims—that the cure for the problems of socialism is more socialism and that the cure for the deficiencies of democracy is more democracy—should be therefore treated not as propositions, but as manifestations of political piety and, to be more terse, of political sanctimoniousness. Democracy serves to create a state of mind where a citizen feels an inner compulsion to emphasize—in public and in private—the absolute superiority of democracy, to dispel any doubts about this superiority, and to delegitimize as an act of reprehensible disloyalty any attempt to consider nondemocratic corrective options, if only in the forms of intellectual experiments. A person with such an attitude to democracy will probably not use the term "utopia," but there is no better word to denote the system he has been taught to revere.

But Churchill's statement can also have another interpretation: "Democracy is not good, but a better system has not been invented." To many people today this sentence is unquestionably true, but it is patently false. Of course a better system *was* invented, and it happened, conceptually, in antiquity as a result of a long debate about the best political regime. It first appeared in Plato's late works and was further developed by Aristotle.

The argument of the ancient thinkers was simple, and it arose from an accurate observation, well-grounded in political experience, that most regimes are defective by being one-sided: that is, by going too much in one direction determined by the specificity of the group that exerts the predominant influence in the functioning of the system. This observation, one could say, anticipated Churchill's view (or rather that Churchill's view reiterated, in a slightly changed form, the classical insight). The ancients distinguished three basic types of regimes: monarchy (one-man rule), oligarchy, called sometimes aristocracy (minority rule). and democracy (majority rule). They regarded each of them as good in some aspects and deficient in others. Each system, then, while being superior to the alternatives, was also inferior to them. For example, the advantage of the monarchy was that it simplified the decision-making process and gave it greater consistency; its disadvantage, among other things, was the danger of tyranny. The advantage of oligarchy was its educational elitism and its disadvantage a possible subordination of the public interest to that of a minority group. The advantage of democracy was its representativeness and its disadvantages anarchy and factionalism.

A possible solution of the problem of one-sidedness was to mix the three types. One could therefore devise a political structure that

combined monarchy, oligarchy, and democracy in such a way that each
would foster the advantages and neutralize the disadvantages of the others. We would then have, for example, a democratic representativeness
but at the same time some oligarchic-aristocratic institutions that would
preserve a form of elitism as well as some form of monarchy guaranteeing
the efficiency of governance. Such combination depended on the ingenu-
ity of the politicians and the character of a particular society, and could
produce a variety of hybrid political forms. When Cicero referred to this
mixed regime, he used the name "res publica." This was the beginning of
a very important republican tradition in Western civilization.

In its modern versions, republicanism moved along complex paths,
sometimes losing the original meaning (especially when used solely as
a shorthand for revolutionary antimonarchism), but the main message
given to it by the ancients was often preserved. The political community
organized as a republic was a structure containing various elements, one
being a democratic component. Even the American system, which today
is regarded as the exemplary embodiment of representative democracy,
was established as a hybrid construction. Some of the Founding Fathers
regarded it as a major problem how to limit the rule of the demos and
secure the proper role of the aristocratic element, whose responsibility
would be the defense and propagation of ethical and political virtues.
Tocqueville contemplated a similar problem, which seemed to him even
more pressing, considering that he saw the advent of democracy as irresistible; in the new times that were approaching it then became a matter
of utmost urgency to inject some aristocratic spirit into an ever more
egalitarian society.

Even in the twentieth century, approximately up to the Thirties, this
hybrid view of political regimes was still quite widespread, although the
word "democracy" started making its rapid career, becoming not just
a description but also the norm. This meant moving away from thinking about political regimes in terms of pros and cons to the idolatry of
one type of political arrangement whose flaws were systematically disregarded. With time, it has become a common practice, unfortunately
rather ridiculous, to compliment certain political conducts and actions
as democratic and condemn others as undemocratic. Sometimes such
labelling may be quite amusing, but its funny side escapes most observers.
So when a politician is criticized for being undemocratic because in the

parliament he disobeys the speaker and refuses to yield the floor, one cannot but laugh. This is a democratic behavior in its purest form, invented in a democracy and having a very long tradition in a democratic history.

At any rate, before it disappeared, giving way to the idolatry of democracy, the concept of a hybrid system known as a mixed regime had played a creative role in political thought and practice, as it prevented the politicians from falling into utopianism. There was no one combination model, and the particular political arrangements reflected national traditions, usually dating from pre-democratic times. Given that France (post-revolutionary) was considered a republic just like England and the Netherlands (despite the last two formally being monarchies) and the United States to a certain degree, the republican formula allowed for a considerable diversity, political experimentation, and a great number of innovations that combined modern elements with traditional ones at various levels of public life. In several decades, this approach to political systems not only completely disappeared from the public consciousness, but was also marginalized by political science. The word "republic" is used today only in the sense of the form of government and any attempts to extend its meaning and to restore its former scope provoke the irritation of political scientists.

Politicians are equally reluctant to use the word "republic" because people tend to associate it with some form of oppressive statism. They definitely prefer the word "democracy," which they have been taught to associate with freedom, openness, and diversity. These associations are wrong, of course, because a republic has a higher internal diversity than a liberal democracy, also incorporating undemocratic institutions (for example, aristocratic and monarchical) and satisfying nondemocratic sensibilities. Liberal democracy is more restrictive, being strongly correlated with egalitarian principles that are quite wrongly believed to generate diversity. The opposite is true: egalitarianism does not tolerate aristocratic and monarchical tendencies, not only in the political structures of the state (which might be understandable), but in any other area of public life. And yet liberal democracy, being the single most homogenizing force in the modern world, creates the illusion that it alone stands for social differentiation.

A liberal-democratic man surrenders to the illusion: he believes—quite wrongly—that he has managed to make his inner self more and more intrinsically diversified and therefore while imprinting his ideas on the world around him, he cherishes a reassuring conviction that through him the world also becomes more diversified. But since in fact he himself dramatically loses his sensitivity to diversity, he is utterly unable to see how by his influence the world around him slowly submerges in an ever more stifling uniformity.

The consequences of this version of Churchill's saying are similar to those of the socialist doctrine: the system is not subject to any criticism. In practical terms this means that one cannot move away from liberal democracy in any aspect or area of life, just as one could not move away from socialism in any aspect or area. And even if such a retreat were actually happening by accident or under the pressure of circumstances, one must not admit it or call it a retreat or even speak and think of it in a way that would suggest a deviation from the liberal-democratic model.

There is a possible counterargument to this. One can say that modern Western political countries are actually hybrid regimes despite the fact that they are called democracies. Their mixed character is well expressed by the name itself. As liberal democracies, they are combinations of liberalism and democracy, which—it can be argued further—retains the original specificity of the mixed regime, although modified in accordance with modern realities. But is it indeed the case? Is liberal democracy a mixed regime?

We do not know exactly when the term liberal democracy entered into a wider usage, but it certainly happened fairly recently. In the mid-nineteenth century, John Stuart Mill wrote how freedom was threatened after the fall of traditional autocracies, particularly by the process of democratization through which a society gained an indirect, but more profound control of the mind of an individual. He argued that a possible countervailing force to this dangerous tendency was liberalism, which would open the space for individual disobedience and eccentricity. In the twentieth century Ortega y Gasset advocated some form of aristo-cratic liberalism, also as a counterweight to a stage of democratization that he called a mass society. In short it was obvious for a long time that liberalism and democracy point in two opposite directions and generate incompatible attitudes. Combining them looked, therefore, like an enterprise well worth undertaking.

The establishment of democracy seems to require an urgent counteraction, more so because democracy, as pointed out by such shrewd observers as Tocqueville and Ortega, was something more than a mechanism for the peaceful transfer of power; it had also an ability to change the whole mindset of society by depriving it of all intellectual and psychological impulses, all social habits and aspirations, however creative and valuable, that did not conform to democratic practices. Those writers used a different language and faced a different political reality than the ancient philosophers, but expressed similar concerns, notably arguing that democracy tends to enslave people's minds through methods that are not easily legible and controllable, yet no less perfidious. "I know no country in which there is less independence of mind and less genuine freedom of thought than in America," wrote Tocqueville in his *Democracy in America*. And when he spoke about limitations on freedom he did not mean the legal constraints to express one's ideas, but rather the pressure to remove from one's mind everything that a democratic society did not give a stamp of legitimacy.

The aridity of the democratic mind could be discerned and deplored at that time because classical education was still in force, providing an outside nondemocratic perspective of evaluation. People educated on Aristotle, Plutarch, and Cicero could not help but notice that rampant democratization was accompanied by the unification of thinking that was an direct offshoot of an antihierarchical conformity, so typical of the democratic man. It might seem, therefore, and it did seem to people such as Mill and Tocqueville, that liberalism functions as a vehicle of an aristocratic factor, along the lines previously indicated by the ancients. By introducing more individual freedom, liberalism could reawaken strong desires for high aspirations and infuse some life into the omnipresent pressure of mediocrity. A wave of liberalism was to encourage an attitude of eccentricity which Mill hoped would stimulate the human spirit to search for the new and the extraordinary. Putting democracy and liberalism together seemed a most promising idea: democracy ensured the overall balance of the entire political order, while liberalism was responsible for enriching the society with individual inspirations to improve things, supporting a human desire for creativity and for change.

The concept of liberal democracy, understood as the mix of democracy and liberalism, is usually explained by contrasting it with the totalitarian democracy. The latter term was popularized by Jacob Talmon, who coined it while analyzing the philosophy of Jean-Jacques Rousseau. The favorite quote with which Rousseau was said to seal his fate as a totalitarian comes from *The Social Contract*, from the passage in which he wrote that the general will is entitled to coerce the individual will to obey because such action constitutes "coercion to freedom." The expression is unfortunate indeed, though the idea behind it is more complex than most critics of Rousseau admit. In any case, wrote Talmon (and subsequently other authors), totalitarian democracy is one in which, in principle, the conflict between the state and the individual should not exist, and in the event of such a conflict, the state has the moral duty to coerce the individual to obey. The people with liberal sensitivity rejected this possibility with indignation, asserting—quite rightly—that it defies the most elementary assumption that freedom and coercion are exclusive. Thus from the onset the liberals emphasized the principle—considered unchallengeable—that in liberal democracy man must not be coerced to freedom because the decision is not that of the government, the church, the nation, or any community but of the man himself.

Of course, the republican democracy, as developed in America and later in Europe, never resembled Rousseau's quasi-totalitarian system, at least in its structural mechanism: they were not ruled by the general will but by political parties and factions, which Rousseau would have considered the exact antithesis of his conception. When Tocqueville, Ortega, and others postulated introducing a more libertarian element in democracy, they were less concerned with the political structure of democracy, but more with its social and cultural content. What they feared was the tyranny of sentiment and opinion and the general gravitation of a democratic society toward conformist mediocrity. Although the introduction of civil liberties, the Bill of Rights, and various legal guarantees could sometimes, but not always, create a barrier against the concentration of political power, this was not really a response to the dangers of democracy that were so accurately identified by the representatives of what I called—for want of a better term—aristocratic liberalism.

★ 6 ★

When we look at the changes in liberal-democratic societies, especially in recent decades, at a time when the republican model lost its impact, we see that what actually happened was not so much the introduction of liberalism into democracy but the democratization of liberalism. The effect proved to be the opposite of the expected. Divergent elements such as the democratic and the aristocratic, where one would offset the weaknesses of the other, were not incorporated into one system. Liberalism did not diversify democracy because it was a different type of liberalism than the one the American Founding Fathers, Tocqueville, and Ortega hoped for: not aristocratic, but egalitarian, and as such it reinforced what it should have moderated. This should not have been a surprise because the original idea of liberalism was indeed egalitarian.

The starting position of liberalism—and at the same time a final perspective—is a hypothetical situation in which relatively independent units cooperate through a system of contracts. The democratization turned liberalism into a doctrine in which the primary agents were no longer individuals, but groups and the institutions of the democratic state. Instead of individuals striving for the enrichment of social capital with new ideas and aspirations, there emerged people voicing demands called rights and acting within the scope of organized groups. These groups subsequently petitioned state institutions and exerted pressure on them to change legislation and political practices; over time, they began to affect judicial decisions by the courts, demanding legal acceptance of their position and acquired privileges. In the final outcome the state in liberal democracy ceased to be an institution pursuing the common good, but became a hostage of groups that treated it solely as an instrument of change securing their interests.

The state, more and more involved in the process of supporting group aspirations, largely lost its general republican character and turned into a conglomerate of the social, economic, cultural, and other policy programs enacted and imposed through democratic procedures. This, in turn, meant that the state had to take over more and more specific responsibilities, far beyond the normal operations of the state apparatus. As the new expectations of the groups had more and more to do with their status and social recognition, the traditional means of the state policy were no longer sufficient. It became necessary to intervene deeply into the social substance—where the roots of status and recognition resided—either through direct political action or indirectly by changing the laws, making appropriate judicial decisions, and adjusting morality and social mores drastically to guarantee equality. The state representatives, armed with the rhetoric of antidiscrimination, felt it was their duty to regulate matters that for too long had remained unregulated, which often meant giving privileges to certain groups and taking them away from others.

Once the liberal democracy became established, those who in the past had complained about the growth of the communist state and compared it with a glorious example of the asceticism of a liberal state could invoke such contrast no longer. The liberal-democratic state—still more effective than a communist state—slowly and steadily underwent a similar expansion and likewise deeply intruded in the lives of its citizens. However, while the communist state's spread and intrusive interference had their source in the determination of the authorities who, in order to survive, had to impose, forcefully, more and more controls of social spontaneity, in a liberal-democratic state the source of this growing intrusion was the citizens themselves, both as individuals and as members of the privilege-seeking groups.

With the democratization of liberalism, the state unleashed a drive for hyperactivity by those groups, which in turn resulted in the hyperactivity of political and legal institutions. The government, the courts, and the legislative bodies were under constant pressure to continue their policy of distributing further privileges and granting further rights. Politicians soon discovered that giving way to this pressure or even preempting it was to their advantage because the continuation of the policy of equality was the best method to acquire electoral votes, to secure democratic legitimacy, and to stay in power. Thus a peculiar race began: on the one hand, the groups were inventing more and more effective means to influence the policies of the executive, legislative, and judiciary branches, and on the other, politicians, lawmakers, and judges were increasingly involved in a competition to see which would be the best provider of the new privileges and rights to those groups.

A growing number of group claims required new legislative and judicial decisions, new rules of all sorts to improve the existing law and to provide it with new and ever more up-to-date interpretations. The

legislatures and the courts struggled tirelessly with the new political reality and often assumed the initiatives themselves in order to strengthen
and legitimize their political role. Reversing this process was impossible.
The withdrawal of the state from some areas would entail reducing the
activity of the government ministers, local officials, parliamentarians,
provincial and regional governors, and others. And such a thing could not
and is not to be permitted because in democratic politics it is in nobody's
interest: the democratic mechanism itself was created not to limit political
activity but to keep it going at an ever-higher speed. Restless acting and
reacting, amending and modifying, initiating and taking over, responding to new challenges and challenging others—all of these have been
perceived by politicians, society, and the media as the proper conduct
according to which the man of politics is to be evaluated.

Naturally, it is sometimes difficult to see the relationship between the
interests of a particular group and those of the state due to the constant
activity of the politicians and political institutions. The state that does
not engage in a flurry of activity or effectively convince its citizens that it
will vigorously hustle and bustle to ensure better conditions for specific
groups, quickly passes into the hands of new parties or new trustees
of political power. The slogan "to change and reform" is repeated during every election, regardless of the economic and political situation.
Oftentimes, the changes are superficial and unnecessary; they complicate
simple things, replace better with worse or a lesser evil with a greater one,
but everyone feels the urge to act, even if the activity is phony.

It is also typical of our time that the growth of the state does not go
along with belief—as exhibited in the past—in its miraculous power. The
state has ceased to be associated with great hopes and is no longer viewed
as a political object of worship. Rather, it appears that with its growing
influence and progressive taking on of new responsibilities, the state has
lost the respect of its citizens. Demands directed at the state are nowadays
expressed in a tone of exasperation and angry impatience rather than with
belief in its charitable omnipotence. It can be considered a paradox that
a liberal-democratic man expects more and more from the state that he
values less and less.

And yet, surprisingly, despite this somewhat cynical view of today's
politics and political institutions, the faith in the absolute superiority
of liberal democracy remains unshaken. The coalescing of liberal and

democratic institutions that we observe today, which contributes to the
notion that liberal democracy has no alternative, is nowhere seen more
clearly than in the European Union. The current EU doctrine explicitly states that it is the ultimate system, a culminating emanation of
"European values," a final stage of the history of the European peoples,
worthy of absolute protection and praise. The countries that break loose
of the process or the politicians who express reservations—no matter how
timidly—are immediately subject to disproportionately harsh criticism.
EU propaganda has it that the ongoing political debate in Europe for two
and a half thousand years has come to an end and that Europeans have
finally resolved all major political problems, not only on an intellectual
level or at the level of the institutions across the continent and globally.
The EU has become the highest arbiter of gauging all political developments in the world and—as the Soviet Union once did—the hope of the
oppressed peoples of all continents.

Not surprisingly, the EU has become a major regulating power in
Europe, and its politicians proudly state that they are responsible for
seventy percent of the national legislation. This legislation is mostly
unnecessary in view of the majority of the citizens but necessary from
the perspective of the European institutions: it confirms their power,
regardless of whether it is beneficial for the people or not. The process of
legislation involves vast numbers of people, organizations, and committees and thus creates a colossal army preparing the ground for subsequent
legislation and—so far very effectively—neutralizing any critics. All this
is submerged in a sea of propaganda and ideology. Every piece of legislative regulation is presented not as a simple organizational or administrative decision but as a step toward something great, for which we,
the Europeans, should be grateful. Every directive, Council document,
resolution, or report of the European Parliament must be accompanied
by boastful rhetoric proclaiming it to be another irresistible proof of the
coming victory of the European project. Even what seems to be an obvious failure is presented as a resounding success. The year 2011, in which
the Euro system collapsed, was, in the words of the President of Europe
(that is, the President of the Council), the annus horribilis—which, he
added, in the future will be considered the annus mirabilis. The communist politicians resorted to the same device: they also categorically
brushed away any suggestion that the system had an inherent weakness,

and kept busy convincing the citizens that a constant struggle with the permanent crisis only confirmed the system's superiority.

Taking for granted that liberal democracy is an ultimate political solution had another consequence, perhaps more disconcerting than others because it contradicted a fundamental assumption of the liberal-democratic doctrine. As we recall, liberal democracy was said to differ from a totalitarian democracy in one crucial respect: in the former the citizens could not be "coerced to be free." It appears, however, that the regime has not only been persistently violating this principle, but exhibiting a powerful tendency to go in the opposite direction.

What we have been observing over the last decades is an emergence of a kind of liberal democratic general will. Whether the meaning of the term itself is identical with that used by Rousseau is of negligible significance. The fact is that we have been more and more exposed to an overwhelming liberal-democratic omnipresence, which seems independent of the will of individuals, to which they humbly submit, and which they perceive as compatible with their innermost feelings. This will permeates public and private lives, emanates from the media, advertising, films, theatre and visual arts, expresses itself through common wisdom and persistently brazen stereotypes, through educational curricula from kindergartens to universities, and through works of art. This liberal-democratic general will does not recognize geographical or political borders. And although it does not have a control center or an executive body, it seems to move forward relentlessly and to conquer new territories as if under a single well-structured and well-organized command following a superbly devised strategy. Legislatures that are free, independent, and accountable only to the voters make laws in accordance with its requirements, and the judges, even more free, more independent, and accountable to no one, issue adjudications as its most faithful servants. The liberal-democratic general will reaches the area that Rousseau never dreamt of—language, gestures, and thoughts.

Through people's actions and minds this will ruthlessly imposes liberal-democratic patterns on everything and everyone, including those who should firmly stand for alternative proposals. The socialists and communists, while defending their position, are trying to prove that they are more democratic and liberal than the liberal democrats: more open, pluralistic, tolerant, inclusive, and enthusiastically devoted to entitlements of individuals and groups, more feminist-minded and non-discriminatory. The conservatives, who, in principle, should oppose the socialists and liberal democrats, quite sincerely argue that they, too, are open, pluralistic, tolerant, and inclusive, dedicated to the entitlements of individuals and groups, non-discriminatory and even supportive of the claims of feminists and homosexual activists. All in all, the liberal democrats, the socialists, and the conservatives are unanimous in their condemnations: they condemn racism, sexism, homophobia, discrimination, intolerance, and all the other sins listed in the liberal-democratic catechism while also participating in an unimaginable stretching of the meaning of these concepts and depriving them of any explanatory power. All thoughts and all modes of linguistic expression are moving within the circle of the same clichés, slogans, spells, ideas, and arguments. All are involved in the grand design of which those who think and speak are not the authors but with whose authorship they deeply identify, or—in case of doubt—from which they do not find strength or reasons enough to distance themselves.

This grand design, its supporters say, should be implemented at all cost because it is believed to bring with itself freedom, autonomy, tolerance, pluralism, and all other liberal-democratic treasures. Therefore, all barriers that block its coming can and must be broken down, also for the benefit of those who put up these barriers. If abortion means freedom, then we should raise the consciousness of those who think differently; force doctors to support this freedom and silence priests so they do not interfere with it. If same-sex marriage means freedom, we should then compel its opponents to accept it and silence fools who may have doubts about it. If political correctness is a necessity of life in the liberal-democratic society, then imposing it is, after all, nothing else but a measure of its emancipation for all. The groups that managed to capture this liberal phraseology and the logic that underlies it—such as homosexuals and feminists—have exerted a disproportionate influence on the government to the extent that the state institutions, including the courts, have taken upon themselves the task of breaking the resistance of less conscious and more stubborn groups—that is, of coercing them to freedom.

Today, those who write and speak not only face more limitations than they used to, but all the institutions and communities that traditionally stood in the way of this "coercion to freedom" are being dismantled. As in all utopias, so in a liberal democracy it is believed that the irrational residues of the past should be removed.

Over the last few decades we have observed legislation that has been passed in the name of freedom and of liberal democracy, but which led, with little social resistance, to a considerable limitation of liberty. Parity and quota regulations are a case in point. Although they are typical egalitarian measures, and as such inherently inimical to freedom, they have been largely accepted as a political imperative of a liberal society. One cannot nowadays appoint an executive or elect a representative, be it in politics, business, or art, without a prior selection according to sex, ethnicity, or some other nonrelevant criterion. Another type of legislation, extremely dangerous and also illustrating "coercion to free-dom," relates to what has been called "hate speech," and still another to "domestic violence"; these phrases tend to incriminate more and more acts of conduct and of speech, allowing for further drastic intervention by the government and the courts in family life, the media, public institutions, and schools. When such laws were being passed in some European countries some time ago, an immediate reaction was far from favorable. Many people and institutions—especially in the United States—voiced an opinion that such measures were Orwellian in nature, in the sense that the libertarian rhetoric was used to cover up coercion, making people believe that freedom is slavery and slavery is freedom. Later on, the adjective "Orwellian" was dropped and more countries, including the United States, adopted similar regulations spontaneously carried by the general will, with more and more support by the people or those who claimed to represent the people's will; anyhow, the citizens did not protest, probably having been convinced that they were witnessing a global civilization of freedom in the making.

A similar pressure is exerted on education in general, the result being a rigorous conformity of thought and conduct—all, naturally, in the name of empowerment of students and teachers. Consequently, teachers, like parents, can do less and less, although most of them probably think that the changes are inevitable, and that never before did they enjoy so much freedom. The real power has been shifting to government officials,

who—ostensibly in order to empower young people—decide how their
minds should be formed, free from the potential subversive influence of
teachers and parents. But then both teachers and parents have ceased to
rebel because over time they also have become part of the great universal
liberal-democratic will, bragging about their sincere and deep devotion
to it. Coercion and spontaneity overlap in an almost perfect symbiosis.
And if there is still someone who has not resigned himself to it, he will
soon be called to order by the government and the courts.

The universities are undergoing the same process, which is most
unfortunate because they were regarded for centuries as free industries
of the human mind. Today, any such belief is clearly in discord with reality. The entire education process has been systematically standardized to
make it as close as possible to the liberal-democratic model, in which
group rights are carefully watched, detailed verification and appeal procedures have been established, and the principle of equality is increasingly
more influential in academic community relations. The humanities and
social sciences have long since declared a keen interest in participating in
the process of liberal-democratic changes and are vigorously supported in
their actions by ministries of education, political associations, and supranational institutions. The liberal-democratic jargon, which so painfully
dominates political life also invaded academic life, which slowly became
a reflection of the entire public sphere. Universities are increasingly eager
to introduce a liberal-democratic regime, which makes the vast majority
of academics convinced that they operate in an institution that enjoys the
greatest freedom in its history. But in fact, freedom is in retreat.

The emergence of liberal democracy at educational institutions
led—as elsewhere—to considerable restrictions of the very liberty that
universities enjoyed previously. These developments are undermining a
long and admirable academic tradition. Of course, in the postcommunist
countries, not much was left to be undermined because the old regime
managed to deal with the academic tradition very effectively—with no
small participation of the academics themselves. Remnants of tradition
were occasionally still invoked as a weapon against the excessive intrusion
of the communist government. Whatever else remained of the old days
was wiped clean by the new order. In an age of an increasing number of
rights, continuous group demands, equality, and officially hunted deviations from the established political line, academic tradition did not stand

a chance. The universities began to resemble businesses on the one hand and liberal-democratic political structures on the other.

Let us note here the disappearance of the academic eccentric, a well-known personality, for centuries almost inseparably associated with the academic tradition and its peculiar atmosphere of the freedom of inquiry and inimitable relations between teachers and students. It is not only the ominous presence of political correctness that makes the life of a dissident unbearable. The functioning of the university itself has become so heavily controlled by procedures, rules, and regulations that all deviations from the routine are strictly controlled. If the legendary professors of old, whose unconventional behavior persists in real or imaginary stories to this very day, suddenly, by some miracle, managed to find themselves at today's universities, they would soon be coerced to submission or disposed of as unruly troublemakers.

The coercion to freedom also occurs in the supranational institutions, in particular in the European Union, which—as I previously noted—considers itself the ultimate product of the liberal-democratic idea. Its coercive policies are not something that happens by accident: they derive from the heart of the European Union and from the logic of integration as it is conceived today. European institutions are supposed to represent European society, which, theoretically, seems quite understandable. The problem is that the EU institutions exist, whereas European society does not. Such a society will—we are told—come into existence some time in the future, but this belief is a part of the EU creed, for which evidence is, to say the least, shaky. But once we accept the basic premise that the existing institutions may act for, and in the name of, the society that is believed to emerge in the future, we give them extraordinary powers far exceeding those that are granted within the framework of an ordinary society. Those institutions tend to ignore the rules followed in nation-states, whose governments cannot ignore them because they are answerable to real societies with real identities and loyalties, not to some fictional futurabilia. The European institutions ignore these rules out of the conviction that by doing so they represent what serves European societies best and what those societies really want, even if they are temporarily deluded by the unreason of national particularisms.

The European Union, in other words, believes itself to be a vanguard in relation to the rest of the population, ahead of them in recognizing what is real and what is fictional, and that on their behalf it is pursuing a goal whose value the public will understand only in the future. A popular EU maxim that is striking in its stupidity but repeated as a sign of great wisdom is that integration is like riding a bicycle: you have to keep going, otherwise you will fall. It thus assumes that two groups exist in the EU: one that knows the final goal and that it is imperative for the whole process to be carried out, and one that is not cognizant of the final goal, does not understand it, and rejects it to the detriment of itself and others. This second group represents resistance and this resistance must be overcome for the sake of the whole, something the group will thoroughly understand over time when it gets over its own peculiarity and comprehends the full benefits of integration.

Here, we encounter a replication of the well-known pattern found in the theory and practice of communism. On the one hand, there is the party, which knows the ultimate goal of socialism, identifies with it completely, and understands the need for its existence; on the other are the real people who are not yet fully aware of what is good for them and who should be firmly guided toward the final goal, despite their posed resistance. The emergence of such a pattern of thought and practice at the European level (for example, on the occasion of explicitly and unjustly forcing the Lisbon Treaty on all societies) shows that the coercion to freedom has gone very far—so far that it has eliminated several retreat mechanisms.

There is no indication that the EU will break up with these self-destructive and demoralizing practices. The EU mind—yes, there is such a thing—generated such a mental habit that every dissent is considered a blasphemous assault on the very idea of the European Union and the noble principles that constitute it, just as in socialism every dissent was an incomprehensible act of treason that did not deserve to be left unpunished. The European Union has become the guardian of all diseases of the supranational liberal democracy while itself being the most vivid illustration of these diseases. It has led its institutions, actions, and human minds to such a level of dogmatization that any future remedial movements aimed at restoring freedom and reason will have conflicted with it to a higher or lesser degree, in the course of which the EU itself will increasingly sentence itself to play the role of the ancien régime. It is hard to imagine that while producing so much regulatory power, the

EU would suddenly dismantle it and come to the conclusion that integrational abstinence would better serve peace and cooperation than the coercion to freedom. The emergence of such beliefs in the EU spheres would encourage a European perestroika—something that the European Union might not survive.

CHAPTER III

★ ☭ ★

Politics

★ 1 ★

Communism and liberal democracy are related by a similarly paradoxical approach to politics: both promised to reduce the role of politics in human life, yet induced politicization on a scale unknown in previous history. The most famous statements about the imminent twilight of politics come from *The German Ideology* by Marx and Engels and Lenin's *The State and Revolution*. Marx and Engels imagined how in the world to come man, liberated from the burden of politics, would hunt in the morning, go fishing at noon, and engage in literary criticism after dinner. Lenin predicted a withering away of the state, which would eventually be limited to simple administrative functions. A famous thought attributed to him is that the administration of the communist state would be so simple that "even a kitchen maid" would be able to handle it.

All these stories about a stateless and depoliticized society were articulated in the language of communist eschatology, but in the communist reality things looked different: neither the power-wielding politicians nor citizens trying to find their place in the communist state treated such declarations seriously. The state did not wither away, nor was it likely to do so; citizens' lives were full of politics and no one ever thought of spending their entire life in moving from poetry to fishing and back. And, needless to say, the state's administration was not simplified to kitchen maid level. Such a nonpolitical world did not exist and there was no indication it would ever arise. Rather, we witnessed an almost absolute domination by the Communist Party and, consequently, the growing intrusion of politics into the smallest sectors of what was officially called the "developed socialist society."

Politics remained the sole domain of the Party, primarily its highest authorities, above whom there were the Soviet leaders as the ultimate political sovereign. For the rest of the public, politics meant only an unceasing support for the Communist Party through participation in parades, demonstrations, mass meetings, and other organized outbursts of political enthusiasm. This was politics in a good sense. But politics in a bad sense was also possible. It meant challenging the decisions of the authorities, as, for instance, was done by the Solidarity movement in Poland. This type of "meddling in politics" (as it was then called) was condemned, and often punished by law.

Was communism without politics doctrinally possible at all? At least one important factor negates this possibility: the idea of the class struggle, which in the Marxian theory was to account for the rate and direction of social change. The idea was simple and catchy, with great potential for practical application, though on closer scrutiny it could be easily refuted. As we know, Marx and Engels began by formulating a fundamental class conflict within capitalism, which, according to them, played out between the capitalists, representing the bourgeoisie, and the proletariat, representing the working class. The division of society into two classes seemed to the communists, at some point, a strikingly apt depiction of the capitalist world. But this moment soon passed, and the communist faith faced its first major trial. The original theory of the class struggle predicted a progressive antagonism between the two opposing groups, whereas what really happened was the reverse: antagonism gradually decreased until at the end it virtually ceased to exist.

Some, naturally, parted with this theory, but others tried to save it by claiming that the disappearance of the fundamental antagonism was only temporary, or, better, that it could never happen because as long as there is social injustice, and as long as there are capitalists and imperialists, the struggle continues, even if many people take it lightly or do not see it at all. Stalin's famous statement that the more the communist society is developed, the more fierce the class struggle becomes, though officially abandoned at some point, retained its validity later on in less sweeping versions. All crises of the communist system—protests, riots, demonstrations, activities of the political dissidents, and anything that slowed down the coming of the world revolution and the victory of communism— seemed to confirm that hostile forces, both domestic and international, continued their war against the forces of progress. Even today, despite the fact that the communist empire crumbled, an international brotherhood of Marxists has survived, whose votaries have never stopped preaching that the class struggle goes on, albeit in new costumes and with the use of new weapons.

The communist eschatology promising the world without politics was not, let it be noted, just a hoax perpetrated by ruthless politicians from Marx and his First International, through Lenin, Trotsky, and Stalin to today's socialists from all continents. The paradoxical concept of socialist politics, where everything is political while everyone dreams of a world free from politics, has a much deeper source and accurately illustrates the paradox of the modern mind. On the one hand, modern man believes that making everything political is the highest form of manifestation of his dominion. Politicization is therefore nothing but a consequence of the fact that everything that happens depends on his decision and that only his decision assigns meaning and value to things. Such was the dominant moral postulate formulated by European philosophy from the beginning of modern times. It had to be expected that man's awareness of his growing power over life, society, knowledge, morality, and everything else would be concordant with the increasing presence of politics: more politics meant more instruments to make use of this power.

But the rising tide of politicization did not eliminate the dream of a world without politics. In fact, one could believe, as did many, that disappearance of politics would be not so much a conscious act of elimination as it would the result of politics ultimately fulfilling its function. The final withering away of the state was to be the ultimate triumph of human aspiration to power. Man's absolute control of everything that relates to him is at the same time the stage where the struggle for power becomes irrelevant and political activity comes to an end. Having reached this stage, man can finally do what was always his desire and the innermost striving of his nature—to create, to follow his dreams, to flourish.

This paradox, however, contains a serious problem. If man reaches fulfilment by increasing his decision-making power, then it seems natural to assume that the desire for power lies deep within his nature. Why, then, should we expect that this desire will vanish in some future system that allows the unfettered realization of human aspirations and free expression of human nature? Why would a revolutionary who led the class struggle against the enemy, fought against exploitation, and saw conflict in every part of life at some point turn into an angler and an art critic indifferent to the issue of the distribution of power, willingly passing it on to a kitchen maid? Was the power that absorbed him for so many centuries only a factor that resulted from accidental circumstances, a factor that in other circumstances might never have played any role?

★ 2 ★

This paradox reveals itself to be much stronger in liberal democracy, which, like communism, had a tremendous share in the process of politicizing modern society while at the same time proclaiming loudly that it was pushing humanity to a politics-free world.

How modern man came to this stage is a somewhat complicated story, primarily because liberalism and democracy, taken separately, had different approaches to politics. For a long time, liberalism was believed to be a theory describing human activity as largely nonpolitical, and a human individual as a private person, not a citizen. A standard illustrator of this view is, of course, John Locke, particularly his concept of ownership and labor. In this view, once the state is created—as a result of a free contract—its main duty is to defend property, whose owners expand it through work; this in turn should strengthen their links with the state, which makes the process of acquisition possible.

Among the thinkers who, so to speak, privatized the citizen, one should also mention Benjamin Constant. In his famous lecture about the difference between the freedom of the ancients and that of the moderns, he argued that to participate in public life (which was the freedom enjoyed by the ancients) ceased to be a priority in our time and had been supplanted by the individual freedom to pursue private goals. In other words—and Constant wrote this openly, although later he somewhat modified his position—people should elect their representatives to political institutions in order for these representatives to provide them with the freedom to take care of private matters. Politics and the state are in the hands of a small service group, replaced and controlled by the elections, while the rest of the people have as little to do with politics as possible; they keep their peace of mind, devoting their time to running their businesses, increasing their wealth and property, enjoying their family lives, and pursuing personal passions and interests.

But the hypothesis that a liberal man is a nonpolitical animal, however probable it may sound, is false and has never been true. As liberalism progressed, the people did not withdraw from politics, much less abolish it, but, on the contrary, continued to empower it with prerogatives it had never had before. This does not mean that Locke and Constant made an erroneous diagnosis of modern society when they stressed the growing importance of private matters. Indeed, these matters soon became the major object of interest of politicians and thinkers. But this did not result at all in depoliticization. The majority of private people did not divest themselves of political passions, and whatever private pleasures they pursued, these goals did not change the inherently political character of a modern society.

And it is easy to understand why. Liberalism is primarily a doctrine of power, both self-regarding and other-regarding: it aims to limit the power of other agents, and at the same time grants enormous prerogatives for itself. In a sense it is a super-theory of society, logically prior to and—by its own declaration of self-importance—higher than any other. It attributes to itself the right to be more general, more spacious, and more universal than any of its rivals. Its goal is—as the liberals say—to create a general framework within which others will be able to cooperate. The liberals will never voluntarily give up this admittedly highest of political prerogatives to anyone and will never agree to share it.

Why this extraordinary hubris and the belief that liberalism should play the main, in matter of fact, the only organizing role in society? Until recently, the liberals have been saying, probably in good faith, that they are doctrinally transparent because not only do they not exclude anyone from the great society but they want to include everyone in it. To use an analogy: they think they are like those who write the rules of the road and at the same time are responsible for directing traffic. They aim to create a system that will be most efficient and most convenient to a large number

of vehicles, much higher than that of other road builders or traffic wardens. According to what they have claimed, they are the only ones who
can create such a system because only they are neutral, their sole interest
being to secure freedom for each and every agent.

This noble goal, however, has its other side, usually ignored by liberals
who claim to be transparent. Not only do these liberals position themselves above the others, but they always demand more power—ostensibly
for making more traffic rules and hiring more traffic wardens—being
almost never satisfied with the power they have. Not only do they want
to control the mechanisms of the great society but also those of all its
parts; not only what is general but also specifics; not only human actions
but human thoughts as well. The original message, "we will only create a
framework for society at large, and you will be able to do what you want
within it" is rapidly turning into increasingly detailed message such as,
"we will only create frameworks in education (in the family, in community life) and you will be able to do what you want within them later." But
even this is not enough: "We will only create a framework at this school
and you will be able to do what you want within it later." Then the class
follows the school and so on and so forth.

Few liberals claim to be transparent nowadays. Most of them openly
stand for a specific worldview, which they believe to be the most adequate
of and for modern times, formulated in opposition to other worldviews
and held to be uncompromisingly superior to them. They no longer hide
themselves under the formula "we are creating only a general framework,"
but fight hard for their power over minds and institutions.

This spirit of partisanship should not be surprising, as liberalism
has always had a strong sense of the enemy, a direct consequence of its
dualistic perception of the world. After all, liberalism is more about political struggle with non-liberal adversaries than deliberation with them.
Although such words as "dialogue" and "pluralism" appear among its
favorite motifs, as do "tolerance" and other similarly hospitable notions,
this overtly generous rhetorical orchestration covers up something entirely different. In its essence, liberalism is unabashedly aggressive because
it is determined to hunt down all nonliberal agents and ideas, which
it treats as a threat to itself and to humanity. The organizing principle
of liberalism—as in all other philosophies aiming to change the world
radically—is therefore dualism, not pluralism. The modern stalwart of

liberalism, Isaiah Berlin, was absolutely faithful to the liberal spirit when he said that the history of human thought could be viewed as a conflict between pluralism and monism, and that liberalism represents the former, whereas everything that is not liberal represents the latter.

This opinion, fairly typical, reveals the absurdity of the liberal claim. First, Berlin and other liberal-minded thinkers put duality—monism versus pluralism, closed versus open, freedom versus authority, tolerant versus autocratic—as the primary division, and by so doing had to assume that whoever supports pluralism must be for dualism. It is like saying that anyone who is for diversity must see the world dichotomously.

This leads to an even more bizarre conclusion: that whoever supports pluralism must favor liberalism, which means that anyone who wants to recognize the multiplicity of social arrangements and the diversity of human experience can accept only one philosophical and political philosophy. Given that in the course of the history of human thought there were dozens of different profoundly nonliberal philosophies—many of them of great intellectual value—such a conclusion can only be compared with Henry Ford's famous statement about the Model T*: in defense of pluralism, we give people the right to choose any available philosophy, provided that they choose liberalism.

Berlin himself, a superbly educated man, knew very well and admitted quite frankly that the most important and most valuable fruits of Western philosophy were monistic in nature. The consequence of this was inescapable: virtually everything intellectually intriguing that the Western mind produced in the field of philosophy had to be classified not only as monistic, but also as nonliberal. Therefore, if we take Berlin's view seriously and disregard all monistic theories in the entire history of human thought, we would be left with very little. The effect of this supposed liberal pluralism would be a gigantic purge of Western philosophy, bringing an inevitable degradation of the human mind.

The communists, who were the first to use, and with much success, the dualistic perspective to fight their enemies, made us accustomed to a certain practice of philosophical polemic: they evaluated the arguments of their adversaries in the light of political consequences. The arguments were to be rejected not necessarily because of their demonstrated

---

* "I'll give customers any color they want, so long as it's black."

spuriousness but because of their political implications for communism: one accepted what served the movement's cause, and one rejected what hindered its construction. Lenin, of course, made this practice his only method of argumentation: every fact, thought, idea, book or person was looked at from one and only one perspective—whether they were useful for or detrimental to Russian communism.

The liberals adopted a similar Leninist practice, though probably they would not find the adjective pleasing. When faced with a statement, or an opinion, or an idea, the first and most important question they ask is whether any of these may be dangerous: that is, whether they may potentially contradict liberal assumptions. Their favorite version of this approach is a slippery-slope argument. It amounts to the following: if one can indicate that this or that idea may sooner or later lead to some harmful practices, the idea should be discarded as politically contaminated. Because most theoretical claims or statements contain an element of unity—which the liberals would call monism—or imply a hierarchy—which the liberals would call domination—these claims and statements can be interpreted as direct or indirect encouragements to some form of political authoritarianism, and immediately become politically suspect. To give an example taken from Berlin, several philosophers made a distinction between superior and inferior parts of the soul. Whether this statement is true or false is of little importance; what is important is that it is politically dangerous because it is easy to imagine a group, a party, a community, or a church considering itself to represent this superior part of the soul and using coercion against another group, party, community, or church to which it will ascribe the role of a representative of the inferior part of the soul. This kind of argument—outrageous, let us admit it—is considered by the liberals to be decisive, and it serves them to disparage opponents by suggesting that by making seemingly harmless theoretical statements they open the gates to totalitarianism, fascism, inquisition, torture, Hitler, and various other horrors.

Surprisingly this essentially intolerant and doctrinaire side has been overlooked, and liberalism achieved a remarkable success in conquering people's minds. In the past few decades, the liberals and the liberal democrats have managed to silence and marginalize nearly all alternatives and all nonliberal views of political order. Liberalism monopolized people's minds to an extent that would put to shame the theorists of socialism in the communist countries, who, after all, had much richer resources at their disposal.

In democracy, politics was perceived in a different way. Depoliticization was not and could not be an ultimate goal. Democracy is the most political of all known regimes: none other engages so many people in civic responsibilities, and none other depends so much on them for its own existence. If the number of participating citizens decreases, the democracy is believed to be falling into a state of crisis and possible delegitimization. If the democratic system is upheld by the activity of a minority, not a majority, it ceases—theoretically, at least—to be democratic, and the entire political mechanism breaks down.

The democratic politicization is of a special kind, being energized by the spirit of partisanship. Modern democracies function on the assumption that the driving force in politics is society's opportunity to choose a program according to which the country should be governed. These programs are presented to the public by a variety of political parties, and the public, through a process of election, selects a party or a group of parties and gives their representatives the mandate to implement the chosen program. As Joseph Schumpeter accurately wrote, democracy is a contest organized periodically by the public to select their representatives. Democratic society is thus political out of necessity because through elections it automatically gets involved in the struggle for power; moreover, this involvement is a civic duty, which the people can renounce only at the price of destroying democracy.

The political mechanism seems almost perfect. Its advantages are manifold: it protects the public from uncontrolled power and provides a right to participate in politics; it secures a smooth transition of power from one political group to another; it offers a wide range of competing programs from which the voters can choose; it keeps the losing parties within the system as they may hope for success in the next election. Of course, in reality the democratic systems strongly deviated from this model in one or more aspects, but it cannot be denied that the mechanism proved formidably efficient in stabilizing the process of transferring power through elections.

The emergence of liberal democracy strengthened the bad sides, rather than the good sides, of the democratic model. The system soon began to limit the offer of the party programs from which the voters were to choose. Of course, the idea that democracy is a system where we, the voters, have broad offerings to choose from—like the customers in a department store—responding to the multiplicity of political preferences, rationally examined by us as individuals and groups, never accorded with the facts. A society might be large, but it need not be diversified. As early as the Athenian democracy it was discovered that the spectacularly noisy conflicts of the bickering political groups did not change the herdlike nature of the demos, and that whatever the initial diversity, democratic tendencies steer society toward some kind of uniformity. Tocqueville, Mill, and a host of others made a similar argument about modern representative democracies.

This phenomenon should not be surprising given the nature of the democratic man: a rather uninspired being, not much interested in the world around him, closed within his own prejudices, and amenable to impulses of mimicry. Democracies have therefore always been threatened by and pushed into uniformity. The mechanism that formed the uniformity of aesthetic tastes, of fashion, with its powerful, often absurd and yet irresistible waves, could be and in fact has been easily extended to the domain of political opinion. True, the party system, which legitimized political divergences, served to counteract this tendency. For this reason representative democracy was considered superior to direct democracy as it was thought to have the tools with which groups could defend their political identity against other groups with different identities.

Unfortunately since the transformation of democracy into a liberal democracy, the spectrum of political acceptability has been distinctly limited. Liberal democracy has created its own orthodoxy, which causes it to become less of a forum for articulating positions and agreeing on actions than—to a much higher extent—a political mechanism for the selection of people, organizations, and ideas in line with the orthodoxy. This phenomenon can be seen especially in Europe, where in the past few decades there has been a major ideological rapprochement of the right- and left-wing parties. This resulted in the formation of what is called "the political mainstream," which includes Socialists, Christian Democrats,

the Greens, Social Democrats, Liberals, and even Conservatives. The
mainstream that runs in Europe today is tilted far more to the left than
to the right. Within it, the left has made a slight shift to the right in some
matters (mostly economic) and made a further move to the left in other
matters (mainly moral), while the right-wing movement's shift to the
left was huge.

Such a process had its roots in the past, even quite distant, but
undoubtedly the single most decisive direct impact came from what
happened throughout the Western world in the 1960s. It was then that a
massive political revolution broke out and brought the left wing to a dominant position. The language of the revolution was a medley of anarchist
slogans, a Marxist rhetoric of class struggle and the overthrowing of capitalism, and a liberal language of rights, emancipation, and discrimination.
Capitalism and the state were the main targets, but universities, schools,
family, law, and social mores were attacked with equal vehemence. The
revolution broke out unexpectedly, considering the fact that the Western
societies were then at the peak of economic prosperity and democratic
stability. To be sure, there existed factors that tarnished this rosy picture
and substantially changed the mood of the public: the European powers'
stormy process of decolonization, America's entanglement in the Vietnam
war, and political awakening of the black population.

The revolution of the Sixties was a success because much of what the
revolutionaries proclaimed was met with widespread sympathy. Many
thought—and apparently they were right—that Europe, indeed the entire
West, had been for a long time harboring the ideas that provided a fertile soil for left-wing movements of the kind that shook the world in the
Sixties. Among the ideas that defined the West's modern identity, shaped
its image of the future, and provided fuel for the revolutions was first and
foremost the idea of equality. As François Furet rightly wrote, equality
gave the West the main moral impulse and determined the direction in
which the political imagination pushed the fighters for a better world.
This paramount status of equality clearly favored the Left much more
than the political Right.

Not only was there a tremendous shift to the left in politics, but this
shift was sanctioned—almost naturally and without much resistance
from intellectuals and politicians—as the spoils of political progress.
A similar shift occurred in the United States, although for specifically

American reasons, a process that has taken place there in the years since is more complex and the left still meets with a major counteroffensive. Therefore, in America we can still see a culture war continuing unresolved for several decades, although the forces of the left seem to prevail gradually over those of the right. Europe has not had such a war, and it is highly unlikely it will break out in the foreseeable future as there is no social force of any significance that could launch an offensive against the cultural monopoly of the left.

It was this formation of a broad political consensus in the Sixties that generated a major influence on the character of the social and institutional changes in Europe. Although the multiparty mechanism continued to induce the parties to assert their own distinct identities against their opponents', the overall degree of diversification conspicuously declined. From that time it has been customary to talk of "mainstream" politics and "mainstream" parties. This qualifying word has become an essential ingredient of today's political discourse and denotes a large, cross-party area of ideas, objectives, and programs shared by the major political forces. The tricky side of "mainstream" politics is that it does not tolerate any political "tributaries" and denies that they should have any legitimate existence. Those outside the mainstream are believed to be either mavericks and as such not deserving to be treated seriously, or fascists who should be politically eliminated.

This process marked a historical change not sufficiently, to my mind, noted and examined. The liberal-democratic system, until then a loose procedural device with two major elements—a multiparty mechanism and universal suffrage—turned into a petrified set of ideas and specific political goals. Moreover, those ideas and goals acquired a strong radical coloring as a result of the 1960s revolution, which profoundly transformed Western societies. The revolution was carried out under the banner of the liberation of various oppressed groups, those who wanted to be liberated as well as those who never considered themselves oppressed. But once the liberal-democratic institutions assimilated these ideas and goals and were forced to assume that their task was to continue this process of liberation through imposing appropriate legal measures and introducing new social norms, they unleashed a rapidly increasing politicization that could not be stopped without rejecting the basic assumption. Whoever dared to doubt that liberal democracy should work for the emancipation of ever-new groups was immediately liable to a charge of being an enemy of liberal democracy as such.

The revolution that shook the Western world in the Sixties did not happen at the time and in the societies of stifling authoritarianism, but, on the contrary, in an era and in the countries where the democratic system was quite firmly established. And yet the rebels were so unhappy with it that they chose to reject it in most inflammatory way, and with it they challenged the existing party system, which—as they claimed—differentiated the political spectrum only superficially, preserving the status quo. This status quo and this arrangement had thus to be broken, but not within the system, but from outside it, through *action directe*. The party system had to capitulate to the will of the people, or rather to the movement that quite arbitrarily assumed the role of the will of the people.

The revolution was not a triumph of classical democracy, but an explosion of livid impatience directed at the discipline of the democratic system. It was no longer acceptable to wait serenely and patiently for the results that democratic mechanisms would bring. It became necessary to fight for a democracy that was more and more democratic as well as more and more liberal, a democracy liberated once and for all from all conservative burdens, a democracy that was certain to bring specific laws, norms, and mindsets. And if it fell short of these aims in any respect, it was generally understood that the system could be manipulated in order to bring what each dedicated liberal democrat considered to be an indisputable benefit. Within a short period of time Europeans changed their perception of democratic politics and became convinced that it was about modernization, progress, pluralism, tolerance, and other sacred aims, which were to be carried out regardless of what the voters decided during elections.

The crowning achievement of these changes in the perception of democratic politics was the European Union, which, after the Treaty of Maastricht, boldly stepped into a new political role, surpassing everything that could be seen so far in the national states.

Earlier forms of European integration were the work of politicians who still had a living and painful memory of the previous war and all its horrors. By launching a plan for integration, these politicians reacted to the experience of the war with its hitherto unknown forms of depravity of human nature and its uncontrolled explosion of political madness. By any standard they were remarkable people, by virtue of their lives and education deeply indebted to what was best in Western culture, particularly its Christian and classical heritage. While it is true that what they wrote about the future of Europe was sometimes too naïve and unnecessarily idealistic, their writings still impress us with the political seriousness and the gravity of thought that only the best traditions of European culture inspire. Today it is difficult to find public figures of similar intellectual and spiritual stature. When one compares the Founding Fathers of integration with the current EU leaders, one cannot resist an impression that the former belong to a different world of a long time past, hardly recognizable today.

The memory of the war experience that gave birth to the idea of integration wore itself out with time. But the passage of time was not the only, or even the decisive, factor. The war was soon forgotten in Western European countries which, after its completion, were almost immediately caught in the turmoil of decolonization that reoriented the consciousness of the population. And then came the revolution of the Sixties. For the majority of Europeans today, World War II is a closed stage of history, both in terms of individual human biography and because it has been judged to belong to the world of the past with no connection to the present. On the other hand, the revolution of the Sixties is still a living experience, not only in the minds of old men remembering their rebellious youth, but also because its social mythology is still eagerly received and relived by the younger generation.

At some point, the '68 generation finally laid their hands on European integration. The difference between the Founding Fathers and their successors is enormous. The former were—like their philosophical predecessors from Hugo Grotius to Kant—seekers of perpetual peace. In their moments of sentimental nostalgia, they spoke fondly of a European brotherhood of nations, thus resembling the former visionaries of European spiritual unity. Their successors, who took over the work of integration, created the Union in Maastricht, and have been ruling it since, no longer talk about peace or evoke a shared European heritage but seek to construct a federal super-state, to create a European demos and a new European man. They are extraordinarily self-confident and arrogant and have no particular respect for the heritage they do not know and do not intend to learn about. They are bureaucrats and apparatchiks rather than visionaries and statesmen. They were not shaped by the European culture of which they have limited knowledge and toward which they do not bear warm feelings.

The European Union reflects the order and the spirit of liberal democracy in its most degenerate version. If the strongest features of democracy were the elections and its built-in possibility of changing government and its programs, the European Union has done everything possible to reduce this possibility to the minimum. There are no clear mechanisms for the transmission of power, and no institutionalized way for the voters to affect the direction in which the EU should go. The EU Parliament does not create the government and does not have much power; moreover, it is probably the only parliamentary body in the world, not to mention some of the communist and authoritarian regimes, where there is no opposition. Regardless of who wins the elections, the European Parliament's key decisions are made by the same political cartel and the same policy has been continued for years. European government, or rather something that is the equivalent of the government, i.e., the European Commission, did not arise as a result of a decision by the voting electorate but is completely independent of the voters' will. The main functions in the European Union are conducted by people who are not elected and cannot be recalled by voters, who have absolutely no effective political tools.

How then, in times of such brazen and pervasive democratic rhetoric, could such an undemocratic institution be created? Contrary to appearances, answering this question is quite easy if one remembers what was said above. The European Union was not deliberately created as an anti-democratic system to countervail the weaknesses of democracy, but on the contrary, as a hyperdemocratic or hyper-liberal-democratic project. At least since the time of Maastricht it has been in the hands of politicians and bureaucrats who, whatever their party affiliation, consider themselves to be model liberal democrats ready to convert the whole of Europe and even the whole world to liberal democracy.

Consequently, European politicians do not see any problem in singing the praises of liberal democracy while failing to tolerate any deviation from the orthodoxy of the mainstream. Believing themselves to be the embodiment, the quintessence, and the fundamental guarantee of the liberal-democratic order, they consider it obvious that all those who think differently and challenge their authority must be enemies of the order and that fighting them is a just defense. Equally, it is clear to them that the Parliament, where the same cartel has ruled for years and will still rule unopposed for years to come, is a more perfect political construction than national parliaments, where there is usually an opposition, sometimes even from outside the mainstream, which in the next election has an opportunity to win a majority of seats, create a government, and change the direction of policy to a greater or lesser extent. In the EU, a change in policy is always regarded as disaster of unimaginable proportions.

To the European politicians, the fact that the actual direction of EU policy is created by people who do not have an electoral mandate is of no particular importance, because—as they probably assume—these people were selected and anointed by the elite mainstream. European politicians thus fall victim to the same self-mystification as other groups who identified their own behavior with the views attributed to them. They are motivated by a strong belief that they represent the system, which, as is commonly believed, respects diversity, choice, and pluralism, and this allows them to believe that their rule, albeit still performed by the same majority and having only a loose relationship with the preferences of the voters, is also the rule that respects diversity, choice, and plural-ism. So why risk a good thing? Why over-rely on the decision of voters? Referendum—an old traditional solution of direct democracy, which has serious flaws, but is sometimes necessary—has, for some time now, not enjoyed the respect of the EU mainstream.

Forcing the ratification of the Treaty of Lisbon without a referendum and then playing a pretty perfidious game with the Irish referendum are illustrative examples of these politics. Recently, Greece was prevented from holding a referendum on the issues related to its financial crisis. On the other hand, if it is convenient, the EU blasts the governments it dislikes for failing to adopt a new constitution by referendum. Its attack for this reason on Hungary was, of course, outrageous, given the deceit-ful attempts by the Union itself to adopt its own constitution without consulting the people at all.

Even elections—an impeccably democratic institution, it would seem—are not necessarily deemed always desirable. Recently, precedent-setting cases occurred when the governments in two EU countries, Greece and Italy, were changed without elections, only under pressure from the European institutions. As expected, special circumstances—namely, the financial crisis—were indicated to justify such steps, but the bare fact is that what was violated was not a simple rule or custom, but the holiest of the holy principles by which, as we have been made to believe, democracy stands or falls. Sometimes a country may hold elections, universal, fair, and according to all other rules, but the results are against the expectations of the mainstream; then their credibility—in the eyes of the Union—decreases respectively. Cases in point are the reactions of the EU to the government of the Law and Justice Party in Poland and the Fidesz government in Hungary. Immediately after the elections it launched an extremely aggressive hostility campaign. The mind of a model EU politician has been conditioned in such a way that any dissident move to the right from the mainstream must meet with the most severe condemnation.

The EU political system is not easy to define, and there several ways to look at it. It can be, for instance, qualified as a peculiar example of majoritarian democracy, or, to put it in a less neutral way, as a tyranny of the majority. This shows even in the language used by the European politicians. When told that their supercilious disregard for those outside the mainstream contradicts the basic requirements of the liberal democracy they so touchingly praise, they ignore such an allegation as totally devoid of merit; a minority can afford to say what it wants and still the majority has its way without bothering to reply. And if they were to provide an answer, it would be, "We have democracy here. The majority rules." Needless to say, the answer is—to use communist-speak—to be treated dialectically. There are acceptable majorities, such as the cartel that has ruled the European Parliament for many years, and the unacceptable ones, such as Hungary under the Fidesz. The decision as to which is acceptable and which is not is determined by the mainstream.

The European Union can also be described somewhat differently: namely, as a kind of elite government, or better yet, as a liberal-democratic government of the European aristocracy. The word "aristocracy" is used

here in a metaphorical sense, of course, and is specific to a certain group of
people who believe themselves superior to others. This feeling is probably
a remnant of the 1960s, when the leaders of today, being then young and
rebelling against the political order, already considered themselves, as all
revolutionaries do, superior to the slothful masses.

When they were young, these leaders were believed to be the architects of the new world that was to emerge as a result of the revolution;
now, being old, they claim to be the authors of the institutional system
they think is the greatest political success in history. The attitude in both
cases is the same: a hasty and arrogant dismissal of what stands in their
way and what they readily qualify as prejudice and anachronism. In
this respect, the EU leaders and bureaucrats are no different from other
enlightened governments of the past, except perhaps that they manage
to conceal their contempt for the demos.

Both of these portrayals of the EU—as a majoritarian democracy and
as the rule of enlightened aristocracy—seem to contradict the standard
view of what liberal democracy should be, no matter that this view, as we
know, is often mistaken. In reality, both of them reflect well the internal
logic of the system. It is, of course, true that at the level of nation-states,
voters have more to say and tricks similar to those employed by the EU
politicians would be difficult to manage in most member states. However,
the European Union was not established in the Trobriand Islands, but
on the old continent, and fairly adequately mirrors the present European
way of thinking.

The phenomenon of the mainstream—a shift to the left with a simul-
taneous rapprochement between left and right—did not come into being
in Brussels or Strasbourg but in the nation-states. It was also there that
after the revolution of the Sixties powerful political movements were
mobilized to fight against ever-new forms of so-called discrimination. It
was in the nation-states where a program of enlightened liberal democracy took shape with the aim to manage all facets of individual and social
lives, and, at the same time, to deny political as well as moral legitimacy
to everyone who questioned this program; it was there that an avalanche
of legislation was launched to make liberal democracy the only formula
for all institutions and communities. It is true that European societies
were not given an opportunity to vote in referendums on the Lisbon
Treaty, and when they had such an opportunity—as in the case of the

Constitutional Treaty—a few of them voted against it. It is true that the Treaty of Lisbon would have ended up where its predecessor did, in the trash basket, if citizens were allowed to decide independently again. But once the public was excluded from the decision-making process and the entry into force of the Treaty completed without their participation, no major group protested against the unfair and, as it is commonly said, "undemocratic" attempts by their governments and Eurocratic institutions. No protests were voiced on other similar occasions; the public never questioned the rule of the mainstream, and the citizens of Europe, as well as the political parties in Europe, do not exert any particular pressure on the democratization of the Union.

To be sure, it is difficult to import the EU mechanisms into the systems of the member states—a parliament without opposition, or a non-elected government. What prevents this from happening is the existence of old institutions, too deeply embedded in the tradition to be easily removed. But if we were to imagine the creation of a completely new state in Europe today, the dream country of today's liberal-democratic Europeans, most likely it would not differ much from the European Union. It would be ruled by the mainstream. The enlightened majority would not be threatened by anything or anybody from the margin, those outside the mainstream would constitute a sort of museum of antiquities, and any alliance with them would be an embarrassment. In Parliament, progressive parties would enter into polemics with even more progressive ones, competing to grant further powers to various privileged minorities and issuing increasingly bolder antidiscrimination decrees.

It is difficult to predict the future of Europe within the EU model. In terms of the political doctrine, European society at the moment does not exhibit any ardent desire to move away from such a model, even if the inefficiency and arrogance of the Eurocracy is more and more annoying. Perhaps the future will bring some significant movement from within when the arrogance exceeds the tolerable level. There is no doubt that a remedy must start from the nation-states and it is in them where the first impulse of changes should occur: the dethronement of the mainstream and the breaking of the liberal-democratic monopoly. Until this happens, we will have more of the same: the EU will not change by its own will and the majority of Europeans will continue to cling to the belief that, despite the disadvantages, the EU is a more or less accurate emanation of the soul of today's Europe.

There is yet another engine of politicization in liberal democracy. As I pointed out previously, the system has an inbuilt tendency to extend its rule to all areas of life, no matter how small or, one would think, non-political. While it is true that the liberal and democratic traditions did include a vague promise to accept free nonpolitical self-organization of communities and undisturbed flourishing of social life, this acceptance never really went beyond verbal declarations. What invalidated it was a much stronger tendency, both in liberalism and in democracy, to perform a deep political restructuring of society. What actually happened was the opposite of what the doctrine professed: an atrophy of social spontaneity and a hypertrophy of politics.

In the liberal tradition, communities—such as family and nation— were not believed to have independent existence and therefore have always been looked at with suspicion. Liberals never parted with indi-vidualistic assumptions, according to which collective entities had a sec-ondary role, being contractual and provisional constructions. Doctrinally, nothing stood in the way of rebuilding the communities according to liberal rules, which meant free exit and equal rights to everybody, and the empowering of the state with the tools to eliminate discrimination.

Such strong pressure to restructure communities and ultimately to weaken their roles did not exist in the democratic tradition as long as the democratic mechanisms were limited to the emergence, maintenance, and transfer of power in the government. But after the liberal democrac-racy gained strength and matured, all of that changed. One of the main objectives that the elected authority set before itself was liberalization of society: that is, harmonizing the whole of society with the political system. Liberal democrats were guided by a similar assumption as the communists before them: both disliked communities for their alleged anachronism and, for that reason, thought them, because deep-rooted, to be the major obstacles to progress. Both believed that one cannot mod-ernize society without modernizing communities, including rural areas, families, churches, and schools. Just as communism was not possible with families adhering to the feudal-patriarchal system, so liberal democracy is believed to be incomplete and unsuccessful with schools respecting traditional moral and cultural authoritarianism. The arguments are analogous. Just as a person coming from a noncommunist community could not become a full-fledged, dedicated, and efficient citizen of the communist state, so a graduate of a traditional school will never be a faithful and reliable citizen of the liberal-democratic state.

Socialists and communists, let it be noted, have always embraced the notion of community, at least theoretically, to a larger extent than liberals, whom they accused of individualism that falsified human nature. However, while emphasizing the role of the community, they sternly and ruthlessly criticized—just as liberals did—existing communities with long traditions, and after seizing power, brutally destroyed them. Villages were treated with particular aversion because they were seen as the mainstay of tradition. Marx and Engels contemptuously wrote about the "idiocy" of rural life, and their successors did everything to destroy rural communities, which they regarded as strongholds of conservatism and bigotry. The communist regimes systematically did their best to wipe out rural culture while at the same time seemingly defended the peasants as victims of exploitation. This inconsistency was not an isolated case. The communists also effectively destroyed working-class communities, even though in its official program the Party proclaimed itself to be the strongest-ever champion of the working class, which it honored by calling on it to become a history-making liberator of humanity.

The brutal crusade against existing rural and urban communities, against farmers and workers, did not prevent the communists from praising "the working people of town and country" and "the proletariat," terms denoting social entities whose existence was rather doubtful. The communists also exhorted "the proletarians of all countries" to unite in the mission of carrying out a worldwide communist revolution. The "proletariat" was an abstract term to which no real community corresponded; it was nothing but a requirement of political strategy. The Marxist proletariat existed only so far as it fulfilled the political criteria of the revolutionary program and the only identifying feature of this construct was its political role. By itself, the status of being a factory worker or being unemployed did not automatically make one belong to the "working people of town and country" or the "proletariat."

The politicization of society by liberal democracy developed some-what differently, but had similar effects. When it became largely acknowl-edged that this system was destined not only to secure a smooth transfer of political power from one government to another, but to organize the entire fabric of society, communities became a natural object of, first, cri-tique, and then, open attack, because they were seen as power structures of an alien nonliberal and nondemocratic nature. Stripped of all content and all value and reduced to the political form, they were forced to accept liberal-democratic rules as the only acceptable standards. Whenever they have managed to resist such standards or have been defended on non-political grounds, they provoked even louder protests. The pure liberal democrats could not but see in them morally outrageous and politically dangerous anachronisms that were to open the door for dictatorship.

The old communal bonds, incomprehensible to and feared by the liberal-democratic mind, were to be replaced with new modern ones. The feminist ideology, for example, proclaimed that women are united by a special feeling of togetherness and solidarity, which they, unsurprisingly, called a bond of sisterhood. It does not require much perceptiveness to see that the women thus defined were a close equivalent of Marx's pro-letariat. Like the proletariat, the women-sisters were believed to form an international, or rather transnational political group whose primary reason of being is empowerment of their entire sex and liberation of all possible chains imposed on them by history and by men.

Just as the "proletariat," "women" is an abstract concept that does not denote any actual existing community, but only an imagined collec-tive made an object of political worship among feminist organizations and their allies. But the paradox is that this feminist woman, being an figment of political imagination, is considered by the feminists to be a proper woman, a woman in a strict sense, the truest woman, just as for the communists the Marxist proletariat was the truest representative of the working class. By the same token a real woman living in a real society, like a real worker living in a real society, is politically not to be trusted because she deviates too much from the political model. In fact, a non-feminist woman is not a woman at all, just as a noncommunist worker was not really a proletarian.

There are other cases of bringing into alleged existence certain groups by giving them—from above, as it were—a political identity. Probably the most striking example are homosexuals, who by a political fiat gained a status of a transnational movement fighting for power and political influence. Even some ethnic groups exist today only insofar as they are seen by their assigned political role as fighters for group entitlements. Multiculturalism, an idea that has become extremely popular in recent decades, is nothing more than a program to build a society in which there exist not many cultures, but many political identities attached to many real or, more often, imagined collectives. Multiculturalism encourages what is today called identity politics. This term may be misleading. It has little to do with a defense of the rich fabric of societies and their historically constituted communities, but should be rather seen as a program of politicization of certain groups that could radically change the fabric of society.

One would think that such a program is congruent with the logic of democracy, which after all is based on the competition among groups struggling for power. This argument is partly correct and partly fallacious. It is correct so far as it actually points to today's persistent tendency to turn social groups into something like political parties, which, once they become parties, lose their communal character. Women, homosexuals, Muslims, ethnic groups are being perceived as and transformed into quasi-parties, organized from above by the political or ideological leadership and not possessing other characteristics than those resulting from the struggle for power against other groups and no other identity than that provided by this leadership, allowing no ideological dissent. Whoever is not a member of this quasi-party, even though for some reason—be it sex, birth, or color—he should be included, but stays outside its boundaries or sometimes even opposes it, is the enemy, a sellout, and a traitor. A black American who condemns the absurdity of African-Americanism, regardless of his virtues and achievements, is considered as much a traitor to his race. A woman who rejects feminism for its crude and destructive ideological content is a traitor to the sisterhood.

This argument is also wrong in another respect. Obviously, communities are not parties, and a society cannot be divided, like a democratically elected parliament, into parties playing political games and vying for power. The word "multiculturalism," still used today despite numerous criticisms and ridicule, represents yet another hoax that liberal democracy created and that turned out to be surprisingly effective. Both parts of the word misrepresent reality. Multiculturalism is not about culture, but about politics. In fact, they should be "polit" (as in "politburo") rather than "cultur," and "mono" rather than "multi."

Many ingredients of the multicultural cake are not ingredients any more but have become the cake itself. Feminism is not the "culture" of feminists or feminist parties or women, but the political platform espoused by governments, the European Union, and many international institutions; the ideology of homosexuality is no longer in the hands of homosexual activists and their organizations but is a major item in national and global agendas. A nation that would dare to entertain any misgivings in this regard or, for example, include wording in its Constitution—as was recently done by the Hungarians—that marriage is a union between a man and a woman, would be subjected to almost worldwide condemnation expressed in the rhetoric of rage and hatred.

The acquisition of all these catchphrases by the mainstream resulted in—paradoxically—further homogenization of the modern world, the more effectively executed because concealed behind the shamelessly fraudulent rhetoric of cultural diversity. Hence multiculturalism does not avert the progressive politicization of liberal democracies, nor stop the herdlike proclivity of a liberal-democratic demos; in fact, multicultural-ism pushes them to a new level. Never before in human history did we see a similar phenomenon when millions of people, indistinguishable from each other, using the same patterns of thinking, politically homo-geneous and oblivious to any other way of viewing the political world except according to the orthodox liberal-democratic version, are not only convinced of their own individual and group differences and proclaim the unchallenged superiority of pluralism, but also want to enforce the same simplistic and tediously predictable orthodoxy on the entire world as the ultimate embodiment of the idea of multiplicity.

All this undermines and weakens communities—their role and their cohesion—and it is the communities that are the major carriers and strongholds of diversity. They are not the only victims. Politicization, which took over "culture," has also wreaked considerable havoc in the law, making it a particularly effective tool of political or, in fact, partisan pow-er. Again, an analogy with communism is inescapable. Naturally, under communism the degree of arbitrariness and control of the courts by the ruling party were much stronger, but the approach to the law in liberal democracy and the use of law by the liberal-democratic mainstream place it closer to rather than farther from communism. Today's mainstream, like the erstwhile communist ruling class, takes over the mechanisms for creating laws and regards it as its exclusive property to be used for its own goals. The modern state openly, even proudly carries out the policy of social engineering, intervening deeply in the lives of communities while enjoying total impunity, which is guaranteed by its control of lawmaking and law enforcement procedures. A markedly important function of the law, to act as a barrier to political hubris, was lost or significantly weakened. Instead, the law has become a sword against the unresponsiveness and sometimes resistance of society to the policy of aggressive social restructuring that is euphemistically called modernization. The law in liberal democracy—as under communism—is no longer blind. No longer can one envision it as a blindfolded goddess holding the scales to determine guilt and punishment. It is now, as it was under communism, one of the engines that transforms the present into the future and the backward into the progressive. The law is expected to be endowed with an accurate picture of what is going to happen in the future so that it can adjudicate today what will certainly happen tomorrow.

Naturally, politics and law in liberal democracies are fickle, just as the reactions of demos had always been unpredictable. But there are exceptions to this. Politics and law are not blind, for instance, to the fact that not all groups deserve support and not all should enjoy the approval of the mainstream, its laws, and its courts. In liberal democracy, as under communism, there are those who deserve special protection and are therefore honored with special privileges. To this selected circle belong groups officially anointed as oppressed. The status of being oppressed results from the ideological orthodoxy; bestowing it on this or that group is a purely political decision, with no regard to reality. Today, for example, homosexual groups have gained enormous privileges precisely because they have been identified as an oppressed group, the status granted to them for as long as liberal democracy reigns. This somewhat bizarre warmth toward homosexuals is probably fuelled by a persistent attempt to deconstruct family, the institution to which the Left has from the very beginning felt a singular hostility.

Muslims are also privileged to some extent, but for a different reason: partly because of the real fear they arouse in liberal democrats, partly for doctrinal reasons, because granting them privileged status is believed to be the living proof of the viability of multiculturalist ideology, and partly as an exercise in moral masochism, as the attitude toward Muslims is sometimes regarded as a test—undoubtedly not an easy one—of liberal tolerance and openmindedness. But there are also less-fortunate groups, not privileged and often treated harshly, such as Christians, whom the liberal-democratic legislatures and courts clearly dislike.

★ 6 ★

Democratic politicization, being similar to communist politicization, differs from it in one important aspect. In democracy the focus is primarily on the cooperation among groups—a problem virtually nonexistent under communism, in which, as it was claimed, conflicts ceased to exist, and therefore a political system of cooperation was no longer necessary. Liberal democracy, on the other hand, makes cooperation a paramount category and considers itself unquestionably superior in that respect to any other system on the argument—irrefutable in its abstract formulation—that cooperation is superior to aggression and war. We do not have unceasing wars, to be sure, but this does not automatically make liberal-democratic politics a model of cooperation. Nor is it true that the so-called politics of emancipation, recognition, and empowerment of groups is permeated by the spirit of "dialogue," "debate," and "mutual respect." These expressions are, of course, well-rooted in today's discourse—nearly as deeply as "the building of socialism" or "a moral-political unity of the nation" were integral parts of the language of communism. But it does not require much effort to see that the dialogue in liberal democracy is of a peculiar kind because its aim is to maintain the domination of the mainstream and not to undermine it. A deliberation is believed to make sense only if the mainstream orthodoxy is sure to win politically. Today's "dialogue" politics are a pure form of the right-is-might politics, cleverly concealed by the ostentatiously vacuous rhetoric of all-inclusiveness.

The belief that the liberal-democratic system has this wonderful cooperative nature, no matter that practice often frustrates it, is not without consequence. Once this belief is taken to heart, it imposes a particular way of thinking. If politics means a mutually respectful cooperation of parties and the opposite is a conflict that leads to discrimination, unjust domination, and, in the last instance, war, then the establishment of cooperation becomes a political imperative. It is certainly not enough to collaborate at the parliamentary and government levels. Cooperative politics should cover virtually all areas of public life because everywhere the alternative to cooperation is discrimination, unjust domination, and war. Everywhere there are groups being denied their rights and therefore struggling for empowerment, and, more importantly, everywhere there are women, homosexuals, Muslims, gypsies, blacks, and representatives of other groups whom liberal democracy gave the status of political quasi-parties and upon whom it thrust the duty of settling scores with the alleged oppressors. Thus everywhere we encounter circumstances that make us aware of the need for cooperation and of the securing the conditions that make it possible.

The success in establishing these conditions at the legislative, governmental, or international levels depends in no small measure—as has been emphatically pointed out—on success in creating such conditions at lower levels. If no dialogue, no tolerance, or no respect for equal rights exists in everything that constitutes a society, even its small and seemingly nonpolitical elements, then all agreements to cooperate politically at upper levels lose their effectiveness. If there is no acceptance of the rights of women and homosexuals in everyday life, in small neighborhoods, then general rules in the Constitution that equate men and women, homosexuals and heterosexuals, are empty declarations.

Effective politics becomes thus a comprehensive task because the preconditions on which cooperation is dependent are not only numerous, but constantly growing in number. Literature, art, education, family, liturgy, the Bible, traditions, ideas, entertainment, children's toys—all can be deemed conducive to cooperation or strengthening intolerance, discrimination, and domination. All contain sentences, ideas, topics, and images that are difficult to accept by some groups and that may be interpreted as reflecting negative perception of these groups. Such negative perceptions, called prejudices, undermine these groups' status, and, consequently, their political position in a democratic society. If in families it is the father who makes the major decisions, then such a power structure in a small social unit generates negative stereotypes that undermine the position of women in the family, which—multiplied by the appropriate number of cases—undermines the position of women in society at large and prevents them from cooperating on an equal footing with men. If a book, for example, Władysław Reymont's *The Promised Land*, presents a picture of capitalists in which their ways of doing business are correlated with cultural-ethnic characteristics—Polish, Jewish, or German—some may consider this portrayal to promote anti-Polish, anti-Jewish, and anti-German stereotypes, which in turn—multiplied by the appropriate number of readers and lessons at school—contributes to serious distortions of cooperation among Polish, Jewish, and German communities in the real world. If people tell "faggot" jokes, then the result—when multiplied by the appropriate number of situations—is the discrimination that intentionally marginalizes the cooperation process for homosexuals as a group.

This explains the rise of the infamous phenomenon of political correctness. There is nothing mysterious about it. It is simply a practical consequence of the view that the duty of citizens of the liberal-democratic society is to participate in the great collective enterprise, where everyone cooperates with everyone else at all levels and under all circumstances. If we look at three above examples—family life, a book's content, and popular jokes—we can see that from the politically correct perspective they are no longer irrelevant trivialities. They illustrate what is absolutely crucial for the entire logic of liberal democracy. Because the logic of this system turns on "dialogue," "respect," "equal rights," "openness," and "tolerance," everything is by definition political, and nothing that relates, however remotely, to these notions is trivial, minor, or irrelevant. A slight offensive remark must always be always regarded as a manifestation of mortal sin. What seems a barely visible mark on the surface conceals underneath swirling currents of hatred, intolerance, racism, and hegemony. The body responsible for ensuring that these terrible things do not surface is the state, with all the instruments at its disposal. It is the state that should incessantly work to impose and improve cooperation policies by removing all real and potential barriers, creating a favorable legal environment, and reshaping public space and education in such a way that the people's minds internalize the rules of politically correct thinking.

Such undertaking carries a high price. When the state takes over responsibility for the rules of cooperation and their enforcement on all layers of society, there will be no limits to its interference in people's lives. The laws it enacts must of necessity be increasingly more detailed and intrusive because what threatens those rules and has to be curtailed is believed to be hidden deeply in social practices and human consciousness. The slippery-slope argument, so often used by liberals, is particularly pertinent here. The logic of liberalism is that whatever seems to be the most obviously nonpolitical, sooner or later will become political. The logic of democracy—with its notions of participation, inclusion, and representation—only strengthened this tendency.

Language was the first to go down this road: initially thought of as potentially descriptive and neutral, it soon came to be seen as the major political weapon used by the oppressors against the oppressed. Thus the faggot jokes are not harmless anecdotes, sometimes funny and sometimes not; the mere fact of using the word "faggot" in speech, public or private, is an act of participation in the exclusion of homosexuals from the democratic cooperation. But because speech is just an expression of thoughts, emotions, and deeply hidden aversions, it must soon become obvious that the actual sources of evil, intolerance, discrimination, domination lie dormant in people's minds, often deposited in their semiconscious layers; uncontrolled and unnoticed, these shape our language and, consequently, our bad habits and negative predilections. These habits and predilections lead to discriminatory laws and authoritarian politics, and in extreme cases, at the very bottom of this slippery slope, to persecution, the stocks, torture, and genocide. But at the beginning, at the very top, is the thought with which it all began—a thought-crime, a mental sin that constitutes the first act of disobedience to holy political principles. Whoever seeks the remedy must start with the political therapy of people's minds.

Communism had a comparably strong sense of political evil, originating—as in liberal democracy—from an internal act of treason and a profound inability to accept the communist message. But the evil could be disarmed or even turned to good once the internal act of treason was disowned and the mind, reborn and reformed, accepted without reservations the communist message. The communist state was not oblivious to this possibility and its functionaries offered various therapeutic programs to help the sinners to abandon bad habits and cleanse themselves of bad thoughts. Once their consciousness was "raised" (as it was then called), they could join good comrades in the march toward the happy future of communism. This—incredible as it may seem—found its continuation in liberal democracy. Even the expression "raising consciousness" was retained, despite its sinister undertone denoting essentially comparable practices of cleansing people's minds of politically subversive mental predilections.

Having gone through consciousness-raising therapy, people could, for instance, rid their minds of sexist thoughts and develop disgust for faggot jokes. America, to my knowledge, was the first liberal-democratic country to create and, in some cases, impose such therapies on people with unruly minds, but the method found zealous imitators elsewhere, including in Eastern Europe. We have already had several enthusiastic reports of some Polish professors who, during their stay at American universities, were shipped, after having sinned, to such a training to have their awareness of a feminist perspective raised. Former patients, equipped with new minds—now politically correct because free from thought-crimes—will probably be the first to be asked to pilot similar programs in their native country in which, as we are constantly reminded by our intellectual pundits, raising the awareness of feminism, homosexuality, and race is of critical importance.

The government is not the only agent that is supposed to oversee the rules of cooperation and fight against all the noncollaborative groups. Actually, this responsibility rests on everyone's shoulders and everyone is responsible for tracking what is wrong and implementing what is right. In this respect, liberal democracy has achieved at least as much as communism and perhaps even more. Real socialism used coercion in the most palatable sense of the word; the authorities treated acts of disobedience with brutality and the bloody birth of the system was not without effect on the behavior of the next generation. In a liberal democracy, a vast part of this process occurs spontaneously, and the legal and political coercion is to some extent a response to public demand and not an arbitrary act of violence against society. Hence the large crowds of individuals who are willing—like some contemporary Pavka Morozovs—to track down dissident words, actions, and intentions in their immediate vicinity. Their Tartuffe-like minds poison the society and other minds.

In liberal democracy, as in communism, a significant role in the task of tracking is assigned to intellectuals who, as the most knowledgeable and enlightened, are best suited for such a task, which is, first, to identify a criminal thought and then to warn against the slippery slope that leads from this thought to political domination. Sometimes this path is not perceptible to a simple mind; it may start, for example, with a noninclusive use of a personal pronoun (he instead of he or she, or, better, she or he, or, still better, she all the time). This use may be indeed a result of simple educational negligence in kindergarten but may sometimes end with the rape of a woman. An intellectual's sharp eye and perceptiveness will always recognize what is politically danger-ous: a sentence, a metaphor, a proverb, an incorrect text on the bulletin board, a work of fiction—a seemingly little thing and yet shamelessly undermining the liberal-democratic rules. And because liberal democ-racy, like communism, produced large numbers of lumpen-intellectuals, there is no shortage of people who ecstatically become involved in tracking disloyalty and fostering a new orthodoxy. It happens that both systems never suffered from a shortage of people willing—often without being asked—to survey the political purity in communities, institutions, groups, and all types of social behavior.

The atmosphere the systems produce is particularly conducive to engendering a certain type of mentality: that of a moralist, a commissar, and an informer rolled into one. In one sense, this person may think that he performs something particularly valuable to humanity; in another, the situation helps him to develop a sense of power otherwise unavailable to him; and in a third, he often cannot resist the temptation to indulge in a low desire to harm others with impunity. For this reason tracking opposition and defending orthodoxy turned out to be so attractive that more and more people fail to resist it.

In both communism and liberal democracy we encounter the same peculiarity: what is incidental is treated as a systemic problem, which really means that whatever happens is systemic and nothing is incidental to the system. It thus becomes natural for true liberal democrats—as it was for true communists—to harass their colleagues because of a casual remark, or of a lack of vigilance, or an improper joke, making the lives of unruly individuals difficult by constantly admonishing and creating further regulations and stricter laws. By doing so, the self-proclaimed guardians of purity see themselves as carrying on their shoulders the responsibility for the future of liberal democracy worldwide. If not for their effort and dedication, this great political enterprise, they think, would become fouled, and then—perish the thought.

As in any system built on violence and lies, in communism this some-what paradoxical belief in both invincibility and vulnerability could be easily explained. It was felt that a few true thoughts and ideas, once they become publicly acknowledged as true, would lay bare the falsehood of the entire structure and eventually tear it down. Even the most self-mysti-fied builders of the structure knew that the truth was their most powerful enemy. And, to speak not entirely metaphorically, it was the truth that tore it down. In a liberal democracy such a view seems absurd because the system is stable and the principle of freedom of speech is included in the Constitution. But those who hunt for political incorrectness and foster political correctness believe or perhaps subconsciously assume that the stability is not as great as naïvely thought nor the freedom of speech as unproblematic as people of ill-will consider it to be.

Under communism the fact that somebody published a poem, a story, a book in an uncensored illegal circulation, or a politically dubi-ous cartoon in a local newspaper, put the entire Politburo on the alert, which sometimes would make the heads roll. Such seemingly small incidents were considered a major problem that would require massive counteractions such as carefully organized demonstrations of workers denouncing the perpetrators, or official condemnations by the associa-tions of writers, artists, actors, and teachers. Just one incorrect word or one word too many was enough to make the creator lose his job or be blacklisted. In a liberal democracy seemingly everything is permissible, but politically incorrect events immediately trigger an avalanche reac-tion of resistance: intellectuals protest, journalists on television twist their faces in moral indignation, comedians use the whip of satire, and the lumpen-intelligentsia, delighted with all that indignation, whistle, heckle, stomp their feet, and demand exemplary punishment of the perpetrators.

A delusion to which the trackers of traitors to liberal democracy readily succumb is their belief that they are a brave small group strug-gling dauntlessly against an overwhelming enemy. And again, an anal-ogy to communism seems irresistible. Under communism people were made to believe that they were involved in a never-ending fight against the enemy. This enemy had various faces and identities, all frighteningly powerful: international imperialism, the CIA, allied reactionary domestic and foreign forces supported by millions of dollars from Washington,

London, and Paris. In a liberal democracy, the fight also goes on and the enemy, too, represents the dark forces, always reviving despite a series of victories by the forces of light: patriarchy, white supremacy, racism, nationalism, and other terrible things said to have millions of supporters and a network of speech and cultural habits established over the centuries. The warriors of political correctness think of themselves in the category of the struggle between David and Goliath. Nothing can be further from the truth. They belong to the mainstream, having all instruments of power at their disposal. On their side are the courts, both national and international, the UN and its agencies, the European Union with all its institutions, countless media, universities, and public opinion. The illusion they cherish of being a brave minority heroically facing the whole world, false as it is, gives them nevertheless a strange sense of comfort: they feel absolutely safe, being equipped with the most powerful political tools in today's world but at the same time priding themselves on their courage and decency, which are more formidable the more awesome the image of the enemy becomes.

The stifling intrusiveness of liberal democracy should not come to us as a surprise once we remember its inner dialectic. Liberalism, as we recall, created a private man and wanted to deliver the vast majority of human race from the burden—unnatural and unnecessary, as the liberals thought—of politics. It succeeded in the first task, and failed in the second. Liberalism, indeed, made people private on an unprecedented scale. Yet these people, having discovered the importance of their privacy, did not renounce politics. Hence when a liberal-democratic man became involved in political activities, it was natural that he imbued them with what he regarded to be the closest to him, what he lived for and breathed and what provided him with the reason for being. But these were matters so far regarded as private. The liberal-democratic man politicized his privacy, perhaps his main contribution to the change in thinking about politics. He politicized marriage, family relations, communal life, language. In this he resembled his communist comrade. But his greatest success in this regard, unmatched so far by any competitor, was to politicize the area that seemed to be the most private of all things private, the most intimate of all things intimate and thus the least appropriate to political meddling: the realm of sex.

Obviously the intentions to politicize sex had appeared before in radical programs aimed at fundamental transformation of society, including the destruction of its traditional institutions. Those radicals and revolutionaries who were looking for a better foundation for a better society knew very well that their program must fail unless they managed to do something with the family. This institution was always considered, quite understandably, to be the most serious obstacle to the task of building a new society. When Plato in *The Republic* raised the question of a perfect political power elite, he naturally related it to the problem of family; he argued that a member of such a true elite should be free from any family bonds because these would weaken his dedication to work for the state, and it was this state that he should regard as his sole object of quasi-familial devotion. To this Plato added a singular politics of sex whose distribution was, on the one hand, give the members of the elite an opportunity to satisfy their sexual needs, and on the other, strengthen the state.

In modern times, the family, while not particularly respected by philosophers of liberal and democratic persuasions, was not an object of a systematic attack. Hobbes, Locke, and Rousseau certainly did not fight against it with the use of arguments referring to sex and sexual instinct. The communists were far more outspoken in this regard. They willingly raised sex arguments to attack the monogamous marriage as an institution. Friedrich Engels, in his work on the family, spoke sharply about the existing institution of marriage, which he compared to prostitution: the wife selling herself upon entering the marriage and the husband buying extramarital pleasures. In his scattered comments, Engels drew a picture of what he considered a good family: the marriage would last only as long as the spouses loved and were physically attracted to each other. It all sounded disarmingly naïve, even sentimental, with no special insight into human nature or the sense of the institution itself.

The idea of "free love" between adults, completely unrelated to marriage, gained some notoriety in the late eighteenth century, and was practiced with little success by some liberally minded eccentrics. It played a more prominent role in the writings of certain communists, who assumed that the communist revolution would inevitably entail a dramatic change in sex mores. Indeed after the October Revolution in 1917 sexual life was set free, with sadly predictable results. Later, this policy was abandoned, mainly because the communist leaders started to perceive it as a whim of the intelligentsia, and militant communism found other fields for action, much more important from the point of view of the revolution. Despite the occasional tide changes, divorce and abortion ultimately became the leading achievements of the new political system and in this regard communism was far ahead of the liberal West.

For the real great sexual revolution the West had to wait until the Sixties of the twentieth century. What happened then was—in terms of scope and content—far more radical than anything in the past. Its consequences, unpredicted during the revolution itself, continue to unfold themselves before our eyes even today, and will most likely continue in the years to come.

This revolution combined two things. First, it repeated the old communist plan to overthrow the repressive power structures, including marriage and family. This time, however—and that was what made it different from previous revolutions—its slogans of sexual liberation mobilized millions of people and it had at its disposal previously unheard-of instruments of ideological warfare, notably mass culture and mass media. The novelty was the clarity of the message: sex was said to be the most powerful element of human nature, and yet still enslaved by oppressive structures from within and from without. This emphasis on sex came probably from Freudianism, which had a particularly strong impact in America but also a considerable sway in Europe. The new crusaders of sexual liberation simplified Freud's views and widely distributed them a politically palatable, rather carefree version. The message that reached the millions was that human sexual impulses had been so far suppressed, that this suppression had been deleterious, and that once sex was liberated, life would be immeasurably nicer.

The concept received its revolutionary form from Herbert Marcuse, who back in the 1950s came up with a theory—a mixture of Freudianism and Marxism—explaining how to combine sexual liberation with a political struggle to overthrow the system. His argument was roughly composed of two elements: the first a rather diabolical image of the modern capitalist world, able to repel and neutralize all the revolutionary movements of change; the second, an interpretation of sex as the only power in man and society, inherently subversive and as yet uncontrolled by the powers that be. Hence, the proclamation of sexual liberation was a call to political collective action, and sex itself became the paramount political weapon. For some time, this diagnosis remained unnoticed and was considered by many to be quite silly. Why would sexual promiscuity be a tool of political struggle? The very idea seemed unworthy of intellectual attention. However, after several years this theory gained great popularity, especially—as is fairly easy to understand—among young people, including the rebellious students on university campuses.

But there was another side to the sexual revolution—alongside the Marxian Freudianism—that was rarely indicated. The sexual revolution was the culmination of growing consumerism in Western societies, which in turn stemmed from the unprecedented prosperity and security that these societies had managed to achieve. Until the 1960s, the growing number of easily available goods did not include sex: this was regulated by existing social practices as well as by the old moral precepts going back to classical ethics. This growing consumerism tended to weaken both social practices and moral precepts, and replaced them with far less demanding and seemingly more natural criteria of a utilitarian kind, pleasure being the principal yardstick to measure the value of human goals. The impressive efficiency of modern civilization accustomed people to expect that their actions would be instantly gratified. Whatever delayed or hindered this gratification was considered unnatural, repressive, incomprehensible, and in the long run unacceptable.

When we look at this mental change from the perspective of the history of philosophy, we can see in it the final—though, thank God, not yet closed—phase of a long process. From the beginning, pleasure was considered by philosophers to be an important part of the human experience, also having a complicated but powerful relation to morality. For twenty-five centuries the nature of this relationship had been the subject of an engaging and often illuminating debate. This debate unavoidably occasioned the use of other concepts, not identical to that of pleasure but somehow related to it: happiness, fulfilment, flourishing, and a few others. At the end of the day pleasure finally outclassed its rivals.

Perhaps the most momentous aspect of this victory was that the concept of happiness—in classical ethics considered one of the central categories—fell out of use and was eventually equated, quite erroneously, with pleasure. Originally happiness was a quality that one could attribute to an entire life, not to its episodes or moments; under no circumstances could one reduce it to pleasure, a short and transient experience. Pursuing happiness meant planning one's entire life so that it had its own moral consistency and internal harmony, both achieved through the inculcation of virtues.

Bringing pleasure to the center of life engendered a different image of human nature. Human beings, in this view, no longer think of themselves in terms of the whole of their existence, but in terms of moments and episodes. It could not be otherwise because there is no such thing as the pleasure of life. One can talk about pleasures and pleasant moments that happen in life, and one can even encourage people to collect those pleasures and pleasant moments, the more the better. But the latter strategy, even if successful, does not predetermine whether this or that particular life in its entirety is or is not happy. It may have many pleasant moments, but these do not automatically translate themselves into a unifying moral scenario, nor make a life fulfilled. To have a fulfilling life it is necessary to give it a durable inherent meaning that may very well coexist with having many pleasant moments, but is in no way a result of these moments, no matter how many. One can, of course, construe one's life as a series of episodes, but this must, to a greater or lesser degree, undermine the sense of continuity of existence, in more extreme cases leading to different identifications, each associated with a different episode. But even if our lives are episodic, our selves are not. Hence the life dedicated to the accumulation of pleasures, but lacking an internal unity, will most likely not be a happy life because a human being cannot renounce his unity without negative consequences.

The sexual revolution is arguably the most extreme manifestation of the episodic nature of man. To surrender one's life to sexual pleasure meant once and for all abandoning any attempt to give one's existence a unifying meaning; this pleasure is, like no other, related to what is short-lived and ephemeral. Many wise men in the history of European thought consistently warned against the effects of the uncontrolled reign of pleasures over human life. In classical ethics pleasures were feared because they not only do not have a self-mitigating mechanism, but are likely, when unchecked, to do away with external mitigating measures. These warnings were not treated with the seriousness they deserved by modern utilitarians. With the growth of consumerism this fear evaporated. As the new rhetoric of sexual liberation declared the existing limitations on sex consumption unacceptable, the time finally came to push the cult of pleasure to a new low. Free sex was not only pleasure; it also stood for spontaneity against soulless technology and productivity; it stood for peace and universal harmony, with no constraints, no domination, no discrimination.

These musings illustrated, as it is easy to see, an old dream, somewhat modified to new realities, of the advent of the era free of politics where individual people would enjoy individual pleasures, unmolested by the state and its institutions. The difference was that instead of trading, gardening, fishing, reading books, and leading family life—these old dreams lost their charms—being a private man meant now primarily indulging in sexual pleasures, occasionally enhanced with narcotic trips. But as before what was intended as a plan to cleanse the world of politics ushered in politicization on an scale unprecedented in liberal-democratic societies. Millions of people were mobilized to act for the better world, and one wave of sexual liberation followed another. Women, homosexuals, lesbians, polygamists, advocates of sexual communes all wanted to have their claims recognized and to contribute to the making of a new society. Sex became both the weapon to destroy the old order and the instrument to forge a new one. Having been elevated to such a high position, it began to penetrate all spheres of public life—education, art, culture, commerce, language.

The sexual utopia did not come about, but sex was politicized and became a part of the official agenda of the state and its institutions. The rebels, without a moment's hesitation, joined the ranks of the political structures and became their functionaries. The consequences of all this, however, were not necessarily quite those that were planned. Once institutionalized and absorbed by the system, sexual freedom permeated law, customs, social practices, schools, educational programs, and public discourse. Since then, the issues of human sexuality, abortion, homosexuality, and so-called reproductive rights have been espoused by the mainstream and begun to be the basic identification marks in liberal-democratic politics. Today, they are supported by the United Nations, the WHO, international tribunals, governments, the parliamentary majority, European institutions, universities, and innumerable think-tanks and non-governmental organizations. Long-haired hippies chanting "make love, not war" have been replaced by today's politicians, teachers, bureaucrats, and lawyers.

The cult of pleasure that once ignited the revolutionary flame does not cause great excitement today. People have more fun and fun is still what people are said to be after, but these pursuits did not bring happiness to human life. Contemporary literature describing the condition of sexually liberated man depicts a rather gloomy picture of despair and senselessness. Yet the existential vacuum in which the modern man found himself after the revolution did not diminish the continued onslaught of sexual politics on society. The institutionalization of sex closed the road that was once opened to man by hedonism, and made void all the promises of what could be found on this road. New promises would sound hollow, as one cannot go further than sex. One cannot indicate other human experience, which would be more basic and more democratic, luring people with more tempting illusions of liberation, giving more intense pleasures and being more correlated with episodic existence. The only thing that can happen to people and societies going along this road is a continuation of the same sexual policy, which, perpetuated by a bureaucratic routine, will become even more ruthless.

CHAPTER IV

Ideology

★ 1 ★

B oth communism and liberal democracy have a strong tendency to ideology. The concept of ideology owes its career to Marxism. Marx and Engels made the following argument. People, they claimed, are not in control of the views they hold and profess; they accept as their own, usually without realizing it, the ideas produced by the socioeconomic system in which they live. Every such system generates not only institutions and economic relations, but also a more or less coherent set of ideas that legitimize it and delineate the boundaries of its change. Contrary to what most of us think, the prevailing opinions, theories, and convictions that we consider timeless and self-evident are neither timeless nor self-evident, but are the product of the economic and political arrangements peculiar to a specific phase of historical development. Whoever thinks otherwise and claims he speaks from a non-committed absolutist perspective is cheating himself, failing to notice that his supposedly politically disinterested consciousness has been fabricated by material conditions. This does not mean that we are all slaves of our time. There are those who see more clearly than others, not because they are free from a historical entanglement, but because their minds have a better grasp of the world to come. It is these people who speak in the name of the future and are the purveyors of a revolutionary spirit. Both these types of consciousness—the one mystified by its false claim to timelessness, the other anticipating a new era—Marx and Engels called ideology.

The concept vaulted to unprecedented popularity, primarily because it proved to be a most convenient tool in political conflicts: it allowed discrediting one's opponent without entering into a substantive argument. There was no sense in analyzing the opponent's views on their merits, such an analysis being usually inconclusive and politically inefficient. It was much better to show that his views represented his interests and were conditioned by his social and economic position. This way, under communism, much of philosophy, art, and literature could be discredited as arising from a bourgeois ideology, legitimizing the domination of the bourgeoisie and representing its interests. By being identified as serving the cause of the bourgeoisie, the philosophers, artists, and writers could be arraigned on a charge of being the enemies of the socialist revolution and standing in the way of the future, often with lamentable consequences for the defendants.

Ideology is always inherently simplistic and simplifying as its function is instrumental, not descriptive. The purpose of ideology is not to disclose intricacies and ambiguities but to make a clear statement: this and this reflect the interests of capitalism, and that and that reflect the interests of communism. Lenin called it, very aptly, the principle of partisanship. One is either for something or against something. Whoever is trying to find a middle-of-the-road position, or to evade the dichotomy, automatically passes to the enemy side. All philosophy—to give a well-known example—is either materialistic, or idealistic. Whoever wants to go beyond this distinction becomes—whether he means it or not—a traitor of the materialist cause and slouches toward idealism.

The ideological interpretation of one of Marx's basic tenets—that the history of humanity is the history of class struggle—stipulated that this struggle leaves its stamp on human life, both individual and collective, on society, art, science, institutions, law. At the peak of communist domination, when culture was in the grip of the doctrine called socialist realism, it was officially proclaimed that nothing in the human world would not have an ideological dimension; in other words, nothing could be neutral with respect to the conflict between communism and capitalism, between the working class and the bourgeoisie, the past and the future. Anything that existed, not only materially, but also as thought or a seemingly harmless folly of imagination, could be non-mistakenly identified as correct or incorrect, bourgeois or proletarian, revolutionary or counterrevolutionary, socialist or antisocialist, materialistic or idealistic, progressive or regressive. This practically put an end to any form of intellectual argumentation. No one argued, but either accused someone of ideological treason or defended himself against such a charge.

No wonder that those contaminated by ideology developed a deep suspicion toward ideas. They knew that ideas were not really ideas, and the person expressing one did not really say what he said—even if he personally thought so—but that he had a hidden agenda, even if he was not personally aware of it. This suspicion increased even more when Marx, who was called the master of suspicion, was joined by two other masters—Nietzsche and Freud.

Nietzsche prided himself on having discovered the genealogies of ideas and disclosed the biological conditions that had generated them: sometimes, he claimed, at their root was strength or weakness of the body; sometimes health or illness (as, for example, skin and gastrointestinal tract diseases were at the root of metaphysics) and sometimes even race (usually, Jewish). Freud, in turn, derived ideas from causal relationships between the conscious and the subconscious minds.

The masters of suspicion practically annihilated a debate understood as an exchange of arguments. When someone expressed an opinion or put forward a thesis, there was no point in considering it in terms of truth or falsehood. It was much better to show, or rather unmask, the conditions that originated this opinion or thesis. One could say, therefore, that the opinion had bourgeois content and served the interests of the bourgeoisie, or that the thesis arose out of ressentiment, or that at the bottom of a certain statement was the Oedipus complex of the speaker.

In the ideological perspective, what looked innocent, whimsical, utterly nonpolitical in art, philosophy, or science, what may have had solely aesthetic, intellectual, or moral value, or no particular value at all, what more or less accurately described the world and human existence, suddenly began to be seen in a new light: all of these were believed to be embedded in a political plan, sometimes all the more insidious because camouflaged. There was not a single writer or artist or thinker who was not ideological, i.e., who would not represent some attitude toward the mechanisms of power, whether affirmative or critical. The communist textbooks and encyclopedias invariably included the information that could pinpoint the ideological identity of artists or authors. Those who were ideologically correct "criticized," "condemned," "exposed," "accused," and "denounced" what it was proper to criticize, condemn, expose, accuse, and denounce. Those on the wrong side of the ideological fence were described as "uncritical apologists," "blind supporters," "sell-outs serving the interests of," "lackeys of the ruling class," "running dogs," and the like.

At some point—actually pretty quickly—the ideology that first served primarily as the instrument to unmask and discredit the false consciousness of those who were the mental slaves of the social and economic environment began to be used as a tool in the service of communism. The new communist ideology had to meet certain criteria: similarly to a capitalist ideology, it had to be so simple and clear that everyone would understand what communism stood for and how to identify an enemy. The difference was that, contrary to the capitalist ideology, the communist counterpart was not false and did not need to be exposed as a false consciousness. Its role was to shape a new mind dedicated to work for a new society. But because this new mind and new society were to emerge through the process of the incessant bombarding of people with a few simplistic slogans, the communist ideology became indistinguishable from communist propaganda. In fact the communists readily admitted it, and used the two words interchangeably: for instance, every Communist Party Committee had its Department of Ideology and Propaganda.

The transition from ideology as a false consciousness to ideology as a true insight into the future of historical development, from the mind full of self-deception to the mind permeated with truth, was quite puzzling. How is it possible, one would ask, that the same person can be, on the one hand, suspicious of all ideas as arising from particular conditions and having no truthful content of their own, and on the other, be dedicated body and soul to a set of ideas that he finds mandatory and compelling? The answer is already included in the question. Ideology is a mental structure that allows a combination of conflicting traits—an extreme distrust of ideas and a blind dogmatism.

The ideological man is thus both absolutely suspicious and absolutely enthusiastic. There seems to be no idea under the sun that he would not put into question and make an object of derision, skepticism, or contempt, no idea that he would not reduce to an offshoot of hidden instincts, mundane interests, biological drives, and psychological complexes. Hence he is likely to despise reason as an autonomous faculty, to downgrade lofty ideals, and to debunk the past, seeing everywhere the same ideological mystification. But at the same time, he lives in a constant state of mobilization for a better world. His mouth is full of noble slogans about brotherhood, freedom, and justice, and with every word he makes it clear that he knows which side is right and that he is ready to sacrifice his entire existence for the sake of its victory. The peculiar combination of both attitudes—merciless distrust and unwavering affirmation—gives him an incomparable sense of moral self-confidence and intellectual self-righteousness.

One should think that liberal democracy is relatively free from ideological temptation. The emergence of one unifying ideology seems rather unlikely when there is considerable differentiation in a society, and it is precisely such a differentiation that liberal democracy promised to tolerate and even stimulate. If, as liberal logic seems to indicate, people are more and more concerned with their private matters; if, following the logic of democracy, political power is available to any party and the democratic pendulum prevents power from staying in the hands of one party for a long time; if, thanks to the efficiency of the liberal-democratic institutions the system acquires remarkable stability and a high degree of prosperity, the need for ideology seems rather insignificant. The ideological propaganda was useful in the communist countries with structural instability and poor economic performance, where it served to disarm people's dissatisfaction and to restructure their minds, by means of aggressive propaganda, in accordance with the directives of the Politburo. But in a country where people are free and prosperous, where they enjoy the rule of law and institutional stability, in a country where human desires are not inhibited and life plans are not regulated, where there is no Politburo and no Department of Ideology and Propaganda, there does not seem to be any place for or need of ideology in the system. Toward which noble goals can human consciousness and the human energy be mobilized? To achieve democracy and freedom? These have already been attained. Bread for all? It's already here and in excess. Universal de-alienation? Who, while living in stable consumer societies characterized by mobility and unlimited access to information and knowledge would be lured by something so ephemeral?

In the 1950s, a number of prominent writers, independently of one another, came up with a widely discussed thesis that the age of ideologies was coming to an end. So said the Americans Daniel Bell, Seymour Martin Lipset, and Edward Shils and Europeans such as Raymond Aron. While they did not foresee the total demise of ideological thinking and even thought that it would continue to be popular among some groups such as intellectuals, they generally saw a conspicuously declining need for and less readiness of societies to be mobilized for a radical transformation by means of simplistic slogans, which, they thought, were irreparably worn out. A liberal-democratic world with a markedly reduced level of ideology seemed a likely prospect.

But soon the experience dealt a blow to these predictions. The Sixties was the time of ideological explosion with the intensity unexpected and unforeseen. A revolutionary rhetoric swept across the entire Western world and awoke a surprisingly strong response. Radical calls to overthrow the system and replace it with another one—unheard of for decades—found millions of sympathetic minds and ears. Even more surprising was that the ideas behind those calls had strong Marxist undertones, and, indeed, were often inspired directly or indirectly by Marxism, the theory that, as some thought, Western societies had long put into the dustbin of history. Intellectuals played a major role in igniting and maintaining the flame of the revolution—and in this respect the sociologists predicting their natural commitment to ideology were right—but mobilization left no segment of society unmoved. Such turbulence the liberal-democratic societies had not lived through for many decades. No institution, social practice, moral rule remained intact.

As one would expect, the new ideology showed its old face: a combination of suspicion and enthusiasm. Suddenly, millions of residents of affluent societies became disciples of Karl Marx, ready to lay bare the dishonesty of the established truths and to search for their economic, political, and biological conditioning. But an enthusiasm was there as well: for the new world, the Age of Aquarius, love, peace, brotherhood, freedom, and spontaneity. The hypnotizing power of the word "utopia"—previously saddled with bad connotations and often associated with inhumane experiments—miraculously resurrected itself.

The feeling that a new utopia was around the corner lasted a few years and then began to subside. But the ideology did not loosen its grip on the Western mind, though the coarse language of the Paris barricades was softened. The flower children quietly retreated from the stage, and so did the Age of Aquarius and the counterculture manifestos. But the society never returned to a pre-protest identity, and there was neither a scenario nor a desire to move away from ideology. Soon the ideology reasserted itself, this time in less menacing form. Now it was the ideology of liberal democracy, slightly more complicated than that of communism, but comparably simplistic and equally impoverishing people's range of thought. The ideological man has colonized a vast part of the public life and private thought, and his conquests are not yet over. As did his communist predecessor, he exhibits a mixture of suspicion and enthusiasm, which gives him a comparable sense of self-righteousness.

In one respect, at least, these ideologies differ, to the disadvantage of liberal democracy. The influence of ideology in communism had a downward trend. At the beginning everything was ideological, but over a long period of time the ideology began retracting—not without resistance, to be sure. For those who lived in these countries it was clear that slowly—too slowly, of course—the ideological vigilance weakened, the crude dichotomies were losing their clarity, the new was fighting the old with less zeal. With the disappearance of the ideological smokescreen reality began to disclose itself in all its richness and complexity. The world, in short, was becoming more and more interesting.

In liberal democracy we have been, unfortunately, observing a reverse trend. The ideological smokescreen is becoming more dense and more impenetrable than before. The entire system seems to have embarked on a great transformation. One would be tempted to say that the system created its own liberal-democratic version of the old communist theory that the building of a new society must coincide with the intensification of the campaign against its enemies. That liberal democracy has ambition to create a new society and a new man, and that it is proud of its achievements, is being proclaimed with deafening vehemence. But at the same time one has the impression that the concluding chapter of this magnificent project is always receding into the future. No matter how much work has been done, the enemy is still as strong as ever. How else one could explain the growing officiousness of ideology? There is more and more of it in politics, in law, in education, in the media, in the language.

Under communism, let us repeat, the conceptual engine that animated the communist ideology was the idea of class struggle, supposedly fought throughout the entire history of humanity. In a liberal democracy, this engine—believed to have been present in the history of humanity since the beginning of time—is an improved version of the original. The Marxists had only "class" as an ideological leverage. In today's liberal democracy the main ideological triad is "class, race, and gender."

But this triad does not exhaust all forces on the battlefield between the old and the new. We have Eurocentrism vs. multiculturalism, heterosexuality vs. homosexuality, logocentrism vs. its opposite, whatever it may be. But even this is not enough. The war goes on between black and white, Africa and Europe, metaphysics and politics, old and young, skinny and fat. We have sexual, ecological, educational, climatic, and literary ideologies, as well as dozens of others. Schools and universities absorb more and more ideology, politics is steeped in it, and the media made it their religion. In the European Union the ideology has been emanating with such intensity that each prolonged contact with its institutions requires a thorough detoxification of one's mind and one's language.

The liberal-democratic mind, just as the mind of a true communist, feels an inner compulsion to manifest its pious loyalty to the doctrine. Public life is full of mandatory rituals in which every politician, artist, writer, celebrity, teacher, or any public figure is willing to participate, all to prove that their liberal-democratic creed springs spontaneously from the depths of their hearts. In the communist system every citizen was expected, regardless of the situation, to mention something—if only en passant—about the absolute superiority of socialism, or a brotherly friendship with the Soviet Union, or the devilish nature of the capitalist exploitation of the working masses; today, in an equal knee-jerk reaction, one is expected to give one's approving opinion about the rights of homosexuals and women and to condemn the usual villains such as domestic violence, racism, xenophobia, or discrimination, or to find some other means of kowtowing to the ideological gods. For instance, it is often advisable to add something about climate change, demonstrating that the outdated term "global warming" is no longer used but at the same time, not even with a quiver of an eyebrow communicating that replacing one word with the other means anything.

This language has practically monopolized the public space and invaded schools, popular culture, academic life, and advertising. This last phenomenon is particularly telling. Today it is no longer enough simply to advertise a product; the companies feel an irresistible need to attach to it a message that is ideologically correct. Even if this message does not have any commercial function—and it hardly ever does—any occasion is good to prove oneself to be a proponent of the brotherhood of races, a critic of the Church, and a supporter of homosexual marriage. This sycophantic wheedling is practiced by journalists, TV morons, pornographers, athletes, professors, artists, professional groups, and young people already infected with the ideological mass culture.

Today's ideology is so powerful that almost everyone desires to join the great camp of progress. This omnipresent urge to seek refuge in this great liberal-democratic church somewhat contradicts the very ideology to which so many have been drawn. If ideology by definition expresses particular interests of particular groups, then the world in which we live should be full of conflicts, or at least of debates in which we would hear the ideological claims of the male part of the population, of Eurocentrists, of heterosexuals, etc. But these claims are not to be heard. Individuals and groups seem to behave contrary to the ideologies they were expected to espouse, but indulge in adulation of the other side; moreover, they seem to do it quite selflessly, out of pure love for the idea, completely ignoring their own alleged self-interest, condition, race, class, and gender.

This created a situation almost as surreal as that under communism. The ideology that was originally to reveal the real roots of ideas—economic conditioning, group interests, biological predilection—turned into an independent agent of such a coercive power that it forced people to say and to do things that, in the light of this ideology, they should not be doing. Men free themselves of male conditioning and become feminists; heterosexuals, supposedly in the yoke of their gender, praise homosexuality most profusely; Europeans, who were said to be the slaves of parochialism, criticize Eurocentrism in the strongest terms possible; philosophers, who for ages have been the apostles of the logos, treat it today with contempt, and the monists have quite unexpectedly became attracted to pluralism and multiculturalism.

★ 3 ★

Political ideology made spectacular conquests in art and intellectual life. Captured by the ideological animus, both socialist and liberal-democratic art abandoned the criterion of beauty—considered anachronistic and of dubious political value—and replaced it with the criterion of correctness. Ideas and works of art had to be ideologically correct. During the dark years of communism, artists were writing books, painting pictures, composing pieces of music that were meant to be straightforward eulogies of what was then called "the correct Party line," including the five-year plans and the heroism of the political security forces in their offensive against foreign and domestic fascists. These artists used their talents to depict, as persuasively as they could, the sinister role of the enemies: the US imperialists, kulaks, spies, and saboteurs. But, as I said, later on, along with the cracks in ideology, art took on a more noble character. In fact, in Poland—and probably in other countries of the region, too—the weakening of communism was accompanied by an extraordinary blossoming of culture, which can only be fully appreciated in our time.

It is, of course, an open question whether there was any clear relationship between the relaxation of the ideological straitjacket and the development of artistic creativity, or whether—which is more probable—this relaxation was simply, as it always is, a necessary, but not a sufficient condition of any free activity including art. Some other factors must also have been present, presumably stronger, yet difficult to identify and certainly impossible to reproduce at will, as is usually the case when at a certain moment of history and in a particular place we have a sudden outburst of artistic creativity. Similarly, it is probably the absence of these or related factors that several decades later prevented the artists of a Poland liberated from communism from reaching comparable heights of artistic achievement, despite the fact that they enjoyed considerably greater freedom both as citizens and as creators of art.

In the liberal democracy of the last decades we have also had a large crowd of artists who produced works meant to be correct: they depict and condemn fascism in all its forms, undermine the center and praise the periphery, call for emancipation and deplore discrimination, declare the superiority of pluralism over fundamentalism, write about the plight of homosexuals among intolerant heterosexuals or women in the world of the merciless patriarchy; they talk of the Other, of sex, of the body. This virtually exhausts the message that the artists of today are conveying to their audience. The message is hopelessly simplistic, but its correctness cannot be doubted, which is enough to give the artists the necessary recognition among the dictators of artistic fashions. The artists who ignore the imperative of correctness have a harder road toward recognition.

Correct art is not only political but in fact apologetic toward the liberal democracy as it is envisaged by its ideology. In this respect, an artist loyal to liberal democracy is no different from an artist who was loyal to communism. Both fight against the enemies of their respective political systems; both oppose what is deemed old and outdated; both take it for granted that the world was a terrible place to live before it became open to the benefits of socialism, in the case of the socialist artist, or of liberal democracy, in the case of the liberal-democratic artist; both tend to depict the human relations as a more or less accurate illustration or a consequence of the political mechanisms—communist or liberal democratic—or the lack thereof; both believe in their respective utopias, at least as a mental exercise or a thought experiment, and both perceive within them the new man to be born by discarding his past conditionings and thus acquiring a freedom to create his identity afresh. To be sure, there are different actors in both cases, and yet they perform similar roles: a proletarian was replaced by a homosexual, a capitalist by a fundamentalist, exploitation by discrimination, a communist revolutionary by a feminist, and a red flag by a vagina.

One encounters a similarly narrow intellectual space in today's humanities, which, ultimately, are dependent on liberal democracy to the same degree that the communist humanities depended on communism. The language they use is not only political, but derived directly from the terminological storehouse of the liberal-democratic ideology: rights, exclusion, recognition, emancipation, equality, domination, colonialism, imperialism, etc. Entering the field of the humanities today—exactly as in the communist past—is like entering into the battlefield: one has to join the forces to defend what is right against what is wrong. Literary critics, writers, performers, filmmakers and theater directors imagine themselves to be listening to the voices of the excluded and searching for the deep roots of domination; anthropologists, social scientists, journalists, and celebrities are preoccupied with pretty much the same, believing—of course—that what they do has a momentous weight upon the world that is, as well as upon the world that will be.

Once we understand how strikingly the liberal-democratic artists and intellectuals are, mentally, a mirror reflection of their communist counterparts, we will notice that the resemblance also extends to the way they behave. In each system the artists and intellectuals willingly gather in herds; they treat dissenters and outsiders with contempt and enmity; they shamelessly enthuse over idiocies that bear the stamp of modernity and exhibit a revolting temerity in the face of what they consider to be the imperatives of the times. Their cowardly behavior they call dignity, and their dishonorable adulation—stupidity, a conscious act of attunement— the spirit of the times. In the past they fell into raptures over the works of the Soviet comrades; today they exhibit ecstatic agitation when reading the works of American feminists, although the intellectual quality is in either case comparably low; in the past they wrote dissertations about Thomas Hobbes as a materialist fighting idealism; today they take Hobbes to be a misogynist defending patriarchy. And even if someone refrained from writing such things then and refrains from writing them now, he would not protest against this sad spectacle of intellectual degradation, not because of his cowardice—to be sure, a widespread weakness among humans in general and the intellectuals in particular—but because in his heart he believes (or is not strong enough to shun the belief) that there must be something fundamentally right in all this deluge of nonsense, and he persuades himself that deprecating it would be more wrong than keeping silent.

Artists and intellectuals often resemble a character in a Polish film who said that he only liked the songs he knew. They, too, reduce every- thing to what they know, being unable to recognize the value of any- thing else. So when they put *Eugene Onegin* on stage, they make the title character and his friend Lenski two homosexuals joined by mutual attraction. This is an absolutely idiotic supposition, but well illustrates what—almost compulsorily—passes for originality today. When they stage *The Magic Flute*, the Queen of the Night becomes the owner of an escort service, obviously a positive character because she represents sex, and sex represents freedom; on the other hand, Sarastro is made into an evil headmaster disciplining students because the headmaster disciplining students today has to be a bad man. In the new productions, Romeo and Juliet are two junkies, and the warriors from Troy nervously wait for a new supply of condoms, and so on, and so forth. All of these examples—real, not made up—are sad proof that artists, supposed to be models of creativity and independence, have come close to being a herd of mediocrities indistinguishable from one another, whose minds have been sterilized of all that is new, revealing, and unexpected.

The authors and artists usually defend themselves by saying that they do all these pathetic experiments mainly for today's audience who find the old texts utterly unrelated to real experience, and who in order to understand those texts need translations into modern cultural idioms. The vicissitudes that befell the Capulets and the Montagues will appeal to modern theatergoers only if the families from sixteenth-century Italy are turned into two gangs in an American metropolis, and if Romeo and Juliet, instead of wearing strange costumes and making long speeches in a funny language, become two junkies or some other characters well-known from the movies and television. These arguments and practices that have trivialized a modern reception of the classical art bring to mind the arguments and practices of the communist artists who—just like their counterparts today—organized themselves into a herd and whose productions were equally predictable. What they were doing was supposedly also for the audience, a different one, to be sure, but equally, as it was then assumed, fed up with the old-style view of literature. So the communist artists modernized the classics to adapt the old stories to the new sensibilities of the communist society. They made Hamlet a progressive political activist, Anna Karenina a victim of class egoism, Antigone a pioneer of the women's movement, etc.

The truth is that the modern artists—no less than their predecessors—make these crude updates of the classics not for the audience, but for themselves. Their works well reflect their imagination and mental capacities, which are just as flat and vulgar. They sometimes try to give the impression, mostly in interviews and press conferences, that this flatness is only apparent, that underneath, their works boil with irony, ambiguity, and a subversive polemics with the old masters, all these being, allegedly, an attempt to bring to light an unorthodox message hidden in the classical literature. Sometimes the artists pretend to be like a character from Gombrowicz's *Ferdydurke* who rebelled against the classics, asking resolutely, "How come they impress us when they do not impress us at all?" However, the same question repeated a thousand times today by the vulgar minds has come to have the value of a television commercial.

Perhaps more adequate would be to compare the artists with their aversion to the classics to another of Gombrowicz's characters, Miętus, known for his notorious fascination with the vulgar and the low. This last analogy may be quite instructive. In *Ferdydurke*, Miętus defeats his adversary, Syphon, a defender of the high and the sublime, by raping him—verbally, that is—through his ears, just as our authors and artists seem to triumph by raping us through our ears and eyes, and above all, through intellect. In Gombrowicz's novel, the episode ends with the death of Syphon, unable to bear the humiliation, and Miętus, during his search for the vulgar, finally, at his own request and to his delight, having his face slapped by a young farmhand. For the time being, today's farmhands, far more cultured than their literary counterparts, kiss the hands of Miętus-like characters, but one cannot rule out that the time will come when they will slap their masters' faces, and not necessarily at their request.

The liberal-democratic man, especially if he is an intellectual or an artist, is very reluctant to learn, but, at the same time, all too eager to teach. This trait of his character is in a way understandable once we remember that his nature was considerably impoverished by his turning back on standards of classical and Christian anthropology. He lost, or rather, as his apologists would have put it, was relieved of the intellectual instruments—deemed unnecessary—that would enable him to describe the inadequacy of his existence and to articulate a sense of want. He is, as Ortega once put it, a self-satisfied individual, not in the sense that he occasionally fails to feel his misery, or to be haunted by a fear of death, a disgust of meaninglessness, a fatigue of the mystification that, as he begins to realize more and more acutely, surrounds him, but because he assumes and never has the slightest doubt that he is in possession of the entirety of the human experience. Looking around, he finds hardly anything that would put this conviction into question and a lot that gives it—practically each day and with each development—a strong corroboration.

★ 4 ★

The ubiquitous ideology in the communist and liberal-democratic societies drag people farther and farther from reality. One of the most unpleasant aspects of living under communism was an awareness that we were always surrounded by nonreality, i.e., artifacts fabricated by the propaganda machine, whose aim was to prevent us from seeing reality as it was. Oftentimes it was a fraud or simply a suppression of information about, for example, the state of the economy, or who murdered whom at Katyń, or what the fraternal Parties agreed on during the summit. But it was something more sinister than that. The entire atmosphere was sultry, because we could not free ourselves from a feeling that we were living among phantoms in the world of illusion, or rather of delusion.

We were surrounded by entities whose reality seemed precarious but whose power of influence was enormous. "Party," "working class," "revisionists," "Zionists," "antisocialist forces," "extremist elements," "five-year plan," "work stoppages," "forces of imperialism," "socialist renewal," "leading role of the party," "fraternal Parties," "domestic export"—all these terms, and many others impossible to translate into English, were supposed to describe real facts, processes, and institutions, but were actually political declarations. It was impossible to conduct any serious debate about the real issues, because the language served to conceal rather than to reveal. Whoever used those key words automatically gave his consent to this function of the language and agreed to take the role of participant in a linguistic-political ritual and thereby to declare his loyalty. The more participants, the noisier the political rites, the more impressive seemed to be the performance of the entire political system in the eyes of those whose minds were limited by the choice of the official language.

The first step in breaking loyalty was to abandon this language in order to see the world as it was, without the mediation of fraudulent words or the false hypostases they generated. This eye-opening experience of a break with the ideological masks and the elation one felt when touching the real world was well-depicted in Polish literature in the 1970s and 1980s. Whoever lived in the atmosphere of those days could not forget this blissful enjoyment of speaking, seeing, and feeling the truth and how, after years of linguistic deception, it brought a breath of life and a reviving influx of fresh air not only to those who dared to reject the language of the ideology, but also, eventually, to the entire community. The mere description of the world, sincere and truthful, had an electrifying effect on people's souls: discovering the richness of human experience, bringing back to the memory long-forgotten facts, the old ideas being revived and restored to their former nobility, recognizing a variety of styles and forms of expression, all of these awakened people from their ideological slumber. Many of them also understood that their newly rediscovered desire to see the world as it was needed to be preceded by the cleaning away of all the contaminating dirt that the decades of ideology had left on their souls.

The collapse of communism and the entry of the liberated countries into the global system of liberal democracy were supposed to intensify and consolidate this change. Europe, or, as it was often said, the West, was believed to be founded on objectivism and truth. After all, it was there where renowned institutions of research and education had flourished for centuries, where free media and free journalists had been giving the world at large free and unbiased information, where science and technology had been developing at an incomparable rate and with incomparable successes, and finally where for decades people had been blessed with democracy, that is, a system with an inbuilt mechanism that allows different points of view to act as correctives to one another's one-sidedness. We thought, or rather we believed, that all these magnificent things would have been impossible without long and institutionalized traditions of respect for the truth and endowing the human mind with a desire for objectivity and an inculcated aversion to ideology.

Those of us who had such high hopes met with disappointment. If the reality revealed itself to us in Eastern Europe, it was short-lived and without consequences. Very quickly the world became hidden under a new ideological shell and the people became hostage to another version of the Newspeak but with similar ideological mystifications. Obligatory rituals of loyalty and condemnations were revived, this time with a different object of worship and a different enemy. The new commissars of the language appeared and were given powerful prerogatives, and just as before, mediocrities assumed their self-proclaimed authority to track down ideological apostasy and condemn the unorthodox—all, of course, for the glory of the new system and the good of the new man. Media— more refined than under communism—performed a similar function:

standing at the forefront of the great transformation leading to a better world and spreading the corruption of the language to the entire social organism and all its cells.

In order to be able to give a fairly accurate description of reality, one has to be somehow detached from it, and it is precisely this condition that the ideology invalidated by transforming the majority of people, whether they agreed or not, into participants in the war it itself created. Practically everyone felt coerced not only to take the right side, but to reassert his partisanship by surrendering to all the necessary language rituals without any critical thought or disarming doubt. The person accused of a reactionary attitude under communism could not effectively defend himself because once the accusation was made it disallowed any objection. Even the best counterargument to the effect that the charge was ill-stated, and that being a reactionary does not mean that one is necessarily wrong just as being a progressive does not mean that one is necessarily right, only sank the accused person deeper. Any such argument was a confirmation of his belonging to the reactionary camp, which was clearly reprehensible if not downright criminal. The only option that the defendant had was to admit his own guilt and submit a self-criticism as self-downgrading as possible, but even that did not have to be accepted. If the defendant had the right to answer the charges in public—and of course he did not—the immediate result was an avalanche of well-orchestrated condemnations and mass protests where the indignant engineers, workers, and writers shredded the insolent reactionary into pieces.

Today, when someone is accused of homophobia, the mere fact of accusation allows no effective reply. To defend oneself by saying that homosexual and heterosexual unions are not equal, even if supported by most persuasive arguments, only confirms the charge of homophobia because the charge itself is never a matter of discussion. The only way out for the defendant is to submit a self-criticism, which may or may not be accepted. When the poor daredevil is adamant and imprudently answers back, a furious pack of enraged lumpen-intellectuals inevitably trample the careless polemicist into the ground.

Prudent people—both then and now—anticipate such reactions and made a preemptive move before saying anything reckless. Under communism, the best tactic was to start by condemning the forces of reaction and praising the socialist progress; then one could risk smuggling in a reasonable, though somewhat audacious statement, preferably wrapped in quotations from Marx and Lenin. In a liberal democracy, it is best to start with a condemnation of homophobia followed by the praise of the homosexual movement, and only then sheepishly include something commonsensical, but only using the rhetoric of tolerance, human rights, and the documents issued by the European Parliament and the European Court of Justice. Otherwise one invites trouble.

The characteristic feature of both societies—communist and liberal democratic—was that a lot of things simply could not be discussed because they were unquestionably bad or unquestionably good. Discussing them was tantamount to casting doubts on something whose value had been unequivocally determined. Under communism, one could not discuss the merits of idealism because by definition it did not have any, or the leading role of the Party because such a role was indubitable, or the good sides of Marxist revisionism because the revisionism had only bad sides, or the controversies over planned economy because there was nothing uncontroversial in it, and many other things that the doctrine declared clearly right or clearly wrong. In a liberal democracy, the degree of freedom is much larger, but even so it seems to be shrinking at a frightening speed. Some concepts are so value-loaded that they permit no discussion, only unconditional praise or equally unconditional condemnation: tolerance, democracy, homophobia, dialogue, hate speech, sexism, pluralism. They therefore serve either as a stick to beat those who are not docile enough, or the ultimate form of laudation. For the majority of people there is no other way but to follow the orthodoxy and to watch one's language. Because the power of ideology increases, one should be more and more careful about the language one uses. The language discipline is the first test for loyalty to the orthodoxy just as the neglect of this discipline is the beginning of all evil.

The liberal-democratic man, just as his communist counterpart, lives in a world almost totally packed with conventions and interpretations, with very little space for individual initiative. He relies almost exclusively on ready-made formulas, moves within well-known stereotypes of thought and language through which he expresses his feelings of approval and disapproval and justifies his role in a community. The ideology that surrounds him is not only a set of concepts but also a system of mandatory practices: like an erstwhile African savage, he is expected to dance his ritual dances in order to manifest his tribal affiliation through the well-trained gestures and rhythms the village sorcerers taught him so that he could express his enthusiasm for the war his superiors thought it rational to wage against the enemies, or to give his joyful support of peace if this accords with the strategy of the tribe. For him there is no reality apart from that which bears the meaning given to it by the sorcerers. Nothing else exists, and if it does, it is not worth communicating.

Of course, one can argue that, after all, in the entire history of mankind, a large part of the human race lived and thought like that; they lived in a world already interpreted and thought according to the rules created by somebody else. But the liberal-democratic society is different from others, being closer to a socialist society than to traditional ones. The difference boils down to two things. The first one was already mentioned: a society that is ideological, that prides itself on having the highest level of emancipation, independence, and autonomy in history, which raises the stark contrast between the declaration and the reality. The second difference concerns the nature of that society: the earlier communities were significantly conventionalized, indeed, but mainly by social custom, not by ideology; today, the custom significantly weakens and ideology takes its place. Ortega was right when he said that in the old societies people had customs, proverbs, stories, and sayings; today they have opinions, which they quite sincerely believe to be their own. What they do not know, however, is that they owe these opinions to the ideology that surrounds them, not to their independent intellectual efforts.

And so, in the absence of social custom and the hierarchy that such custom usually brings about, it is the opinions that today have become the major way of manifesting one's presence in the world. But because we live in a democratic society, the surest way to achieve that goal is to join a large group of people united by having the same opinions. Even if such opinions are stereotyped, expressed in terms of deceptive concepts and in vulgar language full of stale banality that distorts the picture of reality and has a paralyzing effect on our faculties of thinking and perceiving, it is enough that they are shared by a sufficiently high number of people living in the absolute certainty that these ideas are fresh, innovative, and controversially feisty and that their brilliance is worthy of the brilliant minds that emitted them.

★ 5 ★

The overwhelming presence of ideology in liberal-democratic and communist societies can be easily explained. The main cause is equality, which both regimes gave a status of the highest value and made a regulating principle. Both systems enforced the liquidation—through revolutionary means in communism, evolutionary in liberal democracy—of social hierarchies, customs, traditions, and practices that had existed prior to the emergence of the new political system.

The construction of the communist society was possible only after the government carried out a planned and brutal destruction of most of the existing communities and social structures. The new system eliminated the social classes, ostensibly to create a classless society, which in practice meant the dismantling of the entire social fabric—communities, organizations, institutions. In Poland virtually no institution survived—with the exception of the Catholic Church—and the ones that were formally considered to be continuations of the former structures, such as schools and universities, were substantially altered.

In the new society, all people became comrades or citizens enjoying equal status and sharing equal concern for the welfare of communism. This equality was secured and watched by the Communist Party, which had its branches and representatives almost in every segment of society, no matter how small. Alongside a new administrative structure and a new technocratic hierarchy of directors, presidents, and managers, there existed a parallel network of communist committees and apparatchiks who controlled the ideological discipline in the administration and management, setting the goals, nominating the cadres, and preventing any independent decision-making centers from emerging. Universities—to give an example—recreated part of their original academic structures, but next to them, and in fact above them, there was, in each, a Communist Party organization, which made the strategic decisions, supervised academic promotions and the teaching curricula, and saw to it that the central directives were followed.

One can, of course, raise a counterargument to the effect that communism was essentially anti-egalitarian and generated glaring inequalities unparalleled in any other political system of modern times. A member of the party had a far superior status than a fellow citizen outside the party; the top party officials had privileges absolutely inaccessible to ordinary workers. And yet despite all such examples, egalitarianism and despotism do not exclude each other, but usually go hand in hand. To a certain degree, equality invites despotism, because in order to make all members of society equal, and then to maintain this equality for a long period of time, it is necessary to equip the controlling institutions with exceptional power so they can stamp out any potential threat to equality in every sector of the society and any aspect of human life: to paraphrase a well-known sentence by one of Dostoyevsky's characters, "We start with absolute equality and we end up with absolute despotism." Some call it a paradox of equality: the more equality one wants to introduce, the more power one must have; the more power one has, the more one violates the principle of equality; the more one violates the principle of equality, the more one is in a position to make the world egalitarian.

But the root cause of a strong correlation between equality and despotism in communism was of a different kind. In societies that are disintegrated or whose fabric is destroyed by the revolution, political power becomes practically the sole organizing force. Such power does not encounter any resistance, as all forms through which a society normally organizes itself have been wiped out: there are no traditional hierarchies, no spontaneously developed communities, no historically entrenched institutions. When unchecked, despotism meets with no barrier for its self-aggrandizement. This is one of the major reasons why despotism was never effective in traditionally structured societies, where each group, even if situated on a low rung of the social ladder, had considerable autonomy and its own code, hierarchy, and rules of cooperation. Where there are no such groups and no internal differentiation within a society, where there is a social and political vacuum, the despotic power is left as the only form of control. But to be really effective, the despotic control needs something more than sheer terror and intimidation. It must supply the people it has deprived of old social environments with a new identity and a new sense of belonging. And this is the role of ideology.

The communist societies were never made totally egalitarian, although in a country such as Poland it was difficult to indicate an institution—with, as I said, the exception of the Catholic Church—that, during the first ten years of the communist regime, was sufficiently untouched to provide a protective barrier. Later on, some old structures were partially reproduced, but the conquests of social egalitarianism came to be accepted and considered irreversible. The society seemed to have come to a conclusion that equality in itself was a good thing, and that although the means used by the communists were reprehensible, in the end the country was pushed in the right direction. The learned people argued that equality was modernity and that therefore the communists—despicable as they were—served the cause of modernization well. In light of this new logic, what had been once thought to be a barbarism was now viewed as birth pangs of a new society finding its way to modern rationality. The metaphor of birth had another implication: the trend toward more and more equality was one-directional and the hierarchies that were once dismantled or destroyed could not be rebuilt. A desire to reverse the trend would be like a desire for a grown man to return to his mother's womb.

It is true that the egalitarian ideology of socialism/communism sometimes became an object of popular jokes, and its absurd as well as ferocious aspects were not overlooked. Yet the idea that there could be something inherently wrong with coupling modernization and egalitarianism, that equality should not be a paramount value, that ideology was often in costly conflicts with justice, liberty, virtue, beauty, and other basic moral notions, never stayed in the people's minds for long. The value of equality was not only retained unscathed, but turned out to be singularly attractive both as an ethical ideal and a rallying call. No one could legitimately object to the standard of equality because no other standard had behind it the authority of history, ethics, and common sense. To argue that a society should be organized according to a criterion other than equality seemed preposterous. It was therefore quite understandable that if the communist state began to be criticized from within at some point, the most convenient platform for criticism was that it failed the test of equality, the value of which socialism was believed to be the ultimate embodiment but which it unfortunately—for reasons that were never quite clear—betrayed.

But egalitarianism was not only the paramount value of communism. Liberal theories, especially, although not exclusively, those that made use of the concept of the state of nature, assumed people's primeval equality. Looked at from this perspective, all social hierarchies became immediately problematic because they were, obviously, not natural. And because "not natural" meant that they were human constructions, the conclusion any liberal could draw was that there was nothing sacrosanct about them; they could take a different form, be improved upon, or, if need be, liquidated altogether. All inequalities that exist must therefore have explicit justification because otherwise there was no reason for them to be tolerated. Liberalism in the classical version had a clear antiroyalist stance—especially with regard to hereditary monarchy and ancestral institutions, all of which, it was claimed, were based on a "mystification," a reference to mysterious origins in the remote past. This strategy of debunking institutions seemingly ennobled by long history was extended to other social hierarchies—families, schools, and churches—in which one could see, from the perspective of the state-of-nature hypothesis, variations of political monarchism. And once it was assumed that originally we were all equal (no matter that "originally" could have a lot of meanings), it seemed probable that those inequalities that had emerged in the course of history must have resulted from subsequent usurpation, fraud, conquest, accident, and other, similar reasons.

Egalitarian societies have an innate propensity to fall into ideologies, and this for at least two reasons. First, a desire for equality goes hand in hand with a general mistrust toward social and political arrangements, which all, when scrutinized carefully enough, may fail the standard. The feeling of suspicion that they indeed do fail the standard of equality may take a variety of forms. If someone climbs to the top of the hierarchy, no matter if it happened in accordance with the rules agreed upon, he is likely to suspect that those on the levels below him wish to take his place, not because this is the logic of competition, but because the mere fact of somebody's being at the top always offends the egalitarian sensibilities of the rest. The question "why him and not me?" is then an expected reaction of a person with such sensibilities, and the stronger he is, the more painfully acute this question must seem.

Because the suspicion that an unequal distribution of power is immoral and illegitimate increases with the progressive victories of egalitarianism, the struggle for equality has no ending. Equality resembles a monster with an insatiable appetite: regardless of how much it has eaten, the more it devours, the hungrier it becomes. People might generally agree that they are all equal before the law, but this will not dispel the concerns of a dedicated egalitarian, who will argue that this principle is too abstract to be sufficient in every instance. After all, even if we respect equality before the law, other types of inequality and domination continue to exist and their existence is morally repugnant and cannot be tolerated. He will then add that the persistence of inequality and domination has its origin in their being moored in people's customs and habits, which—as can be expected—considerably thwarts the principle of equality before the law. But people's conduct, although entrenched in the historically transmitted experience, has always some deeper sources—in the ways they think and conceptualize their image of the world. So at a certain moment the spirit of mistrust turns to human minds and human thoughts, which are believed to be the fountainhead from which acceptance of the inequalities springs. It is thus a matter of time before the sting of egalitarian ideology is directed against education, where the minds are shaped, against family life and community life, through which human thoughts acquire social durability, against art, language, and science, where they find more refined expression. The spirit of suspicion will not disappear because there are always newer areas to conquer and deeper sources of inequality to discover.

There is another reason why egalitarian societies take ideologies so easily. The experience of communism is, in this respect, illuminating. The communists, who destroyed a great number of the constitutive identities that people had been developing for decades, if not centuries, were aware that the need to belong was deeply embedded in human nature and that the void had to be filled with a new identity. The process of imposing a new identity on the atomized and uprooted mass of people was much more difficult than they thought, but they achieved some success. For many, the new communist identity—though appallingly crude—proved adequate enough to make up for a lost sense of belonging and to give a new one sufficiently strong to create millions of communist sympathizers.

Those who parted, in hope or in despair, with the old homeland, soon embraced the new one and in no time took to heart the rules of the political system, its language, its perverse code of morality, and its absurd mythology. Captured by the imperatives of ideology, they quickly grasped the necessity of being both suspicious and enthusiastic; they knew they had to sever, if only verbally, all links with tradition, and to fill the empty space in their souls with the content of the socialist creed.

Tocqueville brilliantly described the ideological needs of a democratic man. He was perhaps the first to discover how this relatively simple, pragmatic creature, devoid of impractical grandeur and efficient in his activities, is in need of general concepts. This need—he argued—was typical of an egalitarian society in which people are largely undifferentiated, hardly distinguishable from one another because they think in a similar way and are unaccustomed to any complexity of social arrangements or any intellectual ambiguities. Armed with these concepts, they do not want to be bothered with the details or intricacies of the surrounding reality; neither do they have time for complicated intellectual operations or a disinterested cultivation of the intellect. But, of course, they need an overall picture of the world, not only for philosophical self-confidence, but also as a source of ultimate justification for their decisions and their convictions. This is how the democratic man, while thinking of himself as intellectually independent—almost a quasi-Cartesian, as Tocqueville put it—soon transforms himself into a reflection of the social group in which he lives, and submerges deeper and deeper into conformity and anonymity.

The development of liberal democracy confirmed Tocqueville's diagnosis. Because egalitarianism weakens communities and thus deprives men of an identity-giving habitat, it creates a vacuum around them. Hence a desire exists for a new identity, this time modern and in line with the spirit of militant egalitarianism. The ideologies fulfil this role perfectly. They organize people's consciousness by providing them with the meaning of life, an individual and collective purpose, an inspiration for further endeavors, and a sense of belonging. With the emergence of ideology the problem of a lonely individual in an egalitarian society no longer exists: feminism makes all women sisters; all homosexuals become brothers in struggle; all environmentalists become a part of an international green movement; all advocates of tolerance join the ranks of a universal antifascist crusade, and so on. Once a man joins an ideological group all becomes clear to him and everything falls into place; everything is either right or wrong, correct or incorrect. And this perception soon changes the man himself.

In a liberal democracy, as in communism, ideology not only categorizes the entirety of individual and collective existence into correct and incorrect, but also imposes on people's minds an imperative to side with one and be against the other, if not in deed, then in word, or at least in thought. In earlier societies with rich internal structures, differences in loyalty that an individual could experience occurred quite often; in those built on ideology there should be no divided loyalties, and to the extent they exist, they are dangerous symptoms of a deadly disease. The ideological correctness is like a pill that, once consumed by a patient, should improve his organism to such a degree that he must react correctly whatever circumstances and problems he encounters. His mind and body become perfectly united, combining intellectual force with quasi-physiological reflexes, and the moment this unity has been achieved he can no more doubt his wisdom. But because this wisdom turns out to be, in practice, overwhelmingly simple, he cannot help believing that whoever resists it must suffer from some profound malfunction of the mind.

One does not have to be overly acute to see a strong resemblance between a communist activist on the one hand, and a feminist, a homosexual activist, and a liberal-democratic lumpen-intellectual on the other. Their opinions have the same tedious predictability, their arguments are based on similarly crude syllogisms, their styles are similarly vulgar, and their minds are equally dogmatic, unperturbed by any testimony from outside and prone to the same degree of zealousness. On both sides we also see what the Marxists called the unity of theory and practice, which translates into clear language meaning the total subordination of thinking to the ideological precepts of political action; this subordination, instead of being a cause of shame, is proudly held up as an achievement of the new times.

Both sides—communist and liberal-democratic—share their dislike, sometimes bordering on hatred, toward the same enemies: the Church and religion, the nation, classical metaphysics, moral conservatism, and the family. Both are unable to mitigate their arrogance toward everything that their ideology despises, and which, in their revolutionary ardor, they seek to remove from the public space and from private lives. Both are fixated on one or two things that they refer to ad nauseam because those things delineate the unbreachable boundaries of their mental horizon. In every sentence from the Leninist and Stalinist catechisms one can replace "proletariat" with "women" or with "homosexuals," make few other minor adjustments, and no one will recognize the original source. Both sides desire a better world so badly that in order to have it, they do not hesitate to control the totality of human life—including these aspects that are most personal or intimate. Both, unfortunately, have been successful politically and have taken over the ideological power of institutions, laws, and even something as elusive, but nonetheless important, as political atmosphere. It is true that both—those in the communist countries and those throughout the Western world after the demise of communism—were and still are quite frequently an object of jokes, sometimes quite deadly, but at the same time their presence evoked, and the latter case are still evoking, feelings of fear or at least a sense of the clear message that opposing those people is not safe. Finally, both sides had spectacular victories among the intellectual and artistic elites; this is particularly puzzling because one would think that the people endowed with artistic and intellectual talents would be the first to reject with contempt something whose repulsive primitivism only persons with serious mental deficiencies could miss.

The collapse of communism played no small part in making the liberal-democratic ideology more impregnable. The end of the Cold War was almost instantly given an interpretation, and not just any interpretation. No one dared to refute it, despite its obvious falseness. According to it, the Soviet communism that had enslaved many countries in and outside Europe was finally defeated by the West, which represented the forces of freedom and democracy. Millions of people thus accepted the image of liberal democracy as the essence of Western civilization, a system of enormous moral and political power, and an embodiment of the eternal human ideals. This system turned out to be stronger than the great totalitarian empire whose peoples and citizens, having embraced democratic values, made their long dreamt-of vision come true, and could at last go the liberal-democratic way, reclaim their rights, and promote the ideals of pluralism and tolerance.

This picture is patently false. First of all, the liberal-democratic West did not fight the Soviet empire and—with few minor exceptions—never had such intentions. The general strategy of the Western countries was to have good relations with the Soviet Union, even at a comparatively high price. They recognized the empire to be a key player in world politics and part of the political balance on the continent and internationally. Despite occasional heated exchanges with the Soviets, West European governments on both the Left and the Right had mixed feelings about anti-regime movements in the Soviet bloc countries and were far from giving them the endorsement they deserved. The democratic aspirations of the East European peoples posed a risk of destabilization, sometimes to a degree that pushed Europe onto the brink of an international conflict. The Soviets were ready to defend their interests militarily—as in Hungary in 1956 and Czechoslovakia in 1968. The Western powers were aware of this and could not do anything. So it was natural for them to avoid such confrontations, and not to give too much encouragement to dissident activities. They hoped for a durable organic stabilization of the communist system and an equally durable and organic rule of the Soviet Union over its allies-satellites. Such a scenario was far preferable to turmoil in the cause of democracy, or human rights, or any other seemingly sacred principles. The sharper rhetoric and openly anti-Soviet policy sometimes demonstrated by the US government irritated the European politicians, who thought the American politics to be simply immature. If one could imagine the political history of the last six decades without the United States on the political map of the world, and look at communism only through the prism of the relations between the USSR and Western Europe, it seems almost certain that communism would still be thriving, and Poland would continue to be called the Polish People's Republic. From Europe's point of view, conducting the Cold War, much less winning it, was never a priority.

An accommodation between the two parts of Europe was reached at a certain moment, much to the approval of the political elite and the convenience of Western societies. Some communist leaders were believed to have redeeming features—Andropov was fond of whiskey, Gierek spoke French, Kádár invented goulash communism—whereas certain anti-regime movements seemed less trustworthy, especially those that were too conservative and too vocal about their anticommunism. It was obvious from the beginning that among the East Europeans who defied the communist system, those that were closer to the Left found more sympathy and support.

From the point of view of ideology prevalent in Western societies, communism obviously did not have a good image, but the image it had was not the worst. It never incited the indignation that fascism did, the latter term having catapulted to almost diabolical notoriety and denoting the worst of political evil, always placed on the political Right. For this reason anticommunism did not acquire respectability even remotely comparable to that of antifascism. In fact, it was never widely respected, either in America or in Western Europe, or eventually in Eastern Europe after the fall of the old regime. Perhaps the democratic liberals intuitively sensed they had a deeper bond, no matter how unclear, with the communists than with the anticommunists. After 1989 it was obvious what the Western public opinion wanted to hear. No wonder that the moment the communist system fell, the anti-anticommunists and liberal democrats immediately started proclaiming their victory in the Cold War, even if it was the war they had done their best to avoid and during which they had scored a pathetic record of appeasement and pusillanimity. This is what the Western public opinion expected and this is what they got.

To make things worse, when the satellite regimes in Eastern Europe crumbled, the postcommunist leaders and functionaries got amazingly good reviews in the West, as opposed to the avowed anticommunists, who were treated far less kindly. No postcommunist government, even the worst, was condemned by the European Union, while the anticommunist governments—the Polish Law and Justice Party and the Hungarian Fidesz—sparked fury of enormous intensity. To this day, the former and present-day communists are under the protection of the European Union and the political mainstream it represents.

This false image of opposition groups in the communist countries was disseminated and became a sort of uncontested wisdom. To be sure, some of the terms of qualification were partly correct. These groups had been traditionally referred to as the democratic opposition, which, of course, accurately captured what they had striven for: a multiparty system and free elections. The anti-regime dissidents who did not articulate these demands openly kept silent, primarily for tactical, not doctrinal reasons. If democracy stands for a multiparty system and free elections, then all the members of the anti-regime opposition were democrats. But many of them were not democrats in the meaning attributed to the word today. They certainly did not envisage nor were they willing to accept the democratization of the entire society with all its segments, and many of them view the changes in today's liberal-democratic societies with a mixture of bewilderment and disgust.

Another term by which the opponents of the regime were defined was that of human rights. They were routinely called human rights fighters, which, again, was true but in a narrow and frequently misleading sense. It is true that they were fighting for freedom, also for freedoms—of speech, of religion, of research—all of which can indeed by accurately called human rights, not only in terms of the Universal Declaration or of any legislative document, but in a more fundamental sense. It is also true that the anti-regime opposition had no qualms about accepting this term as well as the language in which it functioned because by having done so they obtained a stronger legal justification for their actions and a more efficacious way of communicating their message to the Western public opinion. But it is no less true that most of them were as far as one can be from what today goes under the label of human rights, which is the arbitrary claims, ideologically motivated, made by various political groups in blatant disregard of the common good, generously distributed by the legislatures and the courts, often contrary to common sense and usually detrimental to public and personal morality.

The crucial fact that has been widely ignored is that what gave the anti-regime movements the strongest impetus to resist the seemingly irresistible communist power, and what the communists had tried to eradicate from the very beginning but, to their doom, failed, had little to do with liberal democracy. These were patriotism, a reawakened eternal desire for truth and justice, loyalty to the imponderables of the national tradition, and—a factor of paramount importance—religion. People rebelled because the regime deprived them of what they held the most precious. Free elections and a multiparty system were mechanisms—very much hoped for, nevertheless simply mechanisms—but the massive resistance was not in the name of the mechanism; it was for the ideas this mechanism could serve to achieve. And those ideas were derived from the experience of the nation and, in some cases, that of a religious community. They had nothing to do with the right to democratic schools, or a right to legislation that allows tracking of hate speech, or the right of a teenager to have an abortion without parental consent. If the people who defied communism had been told then that their success would lead to all these things, and all these things would be attributed to their success, they would have felt betrayed. This not because they were not bright enough to see the consequences of their actions, but, on the contrary, because these were the developments their actions were directed against.

Poland's Solidarity movement would not have been possible without its members' strong patriotic and religious motivations. These enabled the Poles not only to rise in large numbers against the oppressive regime, but also to identify the very reasons why they rose against it. These were, among other things, the regime's utter contempt for institutions, laws, norms, and social mores that had both rational and historical justification. To have freedom meant for the Poles not to have a government that would subject these institutions, laws, norms, and social mores to thoughtless social engineering. But this is precisely what happened when the communist regime was replaced by the liberal-democratic one.

The depressing fact was that this sober choice of experience and reason against ideology was not sufficiently durable to withstand the pressure from the new wave of a new ideology. Intimidated and dispersed, the citizens of the new system turned their backs on the old ideals and duly admitted that the credit for defeating the old ideology went not to them and what had really been close to their hearts and minds, but to the new ideology. They readily agreed that liberal democracy was the victor, that it had for a long time animated people's dreams and given them courage to oppose the most inhumane political system in history. It soon turned out that the real victor was even more concrete. When browsing the propaganda materials published by the European Union today, one discovers to one's astonishment that the actual goal of the anti regime opposition in communist Europe was European integration and, indirectly, the then-nonexistent European Union as such.

The amazing propaganda success of this strikingly false interpretation had many unpleasant effects. One of them was a widespread practice of rewriting history and of projecting the stereotypes of the present onto the past. One had an impression that the old ideas suddenly ebbed away, unfairly and prematurely disowned by their former adherents. Many former opposition activists were simply embarrassed by what they had believed in the past, because now those beliefs seemed out of tune with the newest tides of modernity. Even if they were still proud of what they had done, it was now for different reasons, as the old reasons had lost their appeal. The inevitable effect was also a reinterpretation of the political drama that had ended with the collapse of the ancient regime. The old narrative about the national and religious identity reawakened by historical circumstances and by the influence of powerful personalities such as Pope John Paul II had been replaced by a new one, according to which, predictably, there had been a conflict between the forces of light and the forces of darkness, this dichotomy having obviously many analogies—progress vs. reaction, nationalism vs. democracy, liberalism vs. authoritarianism. Who represented the forces of darkness was not clear—the candidates to this role changed together with the evolving of political constellations. What became clear, however, was that a growing number of people started to believe that the real opposition that had defeated the communist regime was a pro-EU one (*avant la lettre*, that is), and that it alone deserved to be honored by the European salons, because it was this group that, together with Gorbachev, the reformist wings of the communist party, the European institutions, Western governments, and the enlightened European public opinion, pushed Europe toward further unification, more pluralism, and more tolerance.

CHAPTER V

Religion

★ 1 ★

For the communist ideology religion has always been a matter of pressing concern. Marx hated religion with all his heart, but at the same time distanced himself from those criticisms of religion, such as Ludwig Feuerbach's, that he thought too crude. Using a quasi-Hegelian argument, he contended that religion would be abolished at some point of a not-too-distant future history, and that with human development coming to its completion it would no longer be needed, and that, when this happened, man himself, in the full bloom of his humanity, would become the proper object of worship.

Marx's attitude well reflects the feelings that the socialists and communists have always had about religion: on the one hand, a profound hostility, often accompanied by an almost sadistic longing for a world in which religion would be wiped out without a trace; on the other, a wish that socialism become a genuine form of religion in the sense that it would satisfy needs, dreams, and desires similar to the way in which religion did and which apparently inhered in human nature. The problem with religion was that, as they said, it satisfied those needs, dreams, and desires in a perverse way, pushing people toward goals that were not theirs, but imposed on them through an ideological manipulation, and ultimately bringing calamities on them and the entire society. But whatever the crimes of religion, its mobilizing power was truly enviable to the socialists and communists, who hoped that once their ideology ascended to a similar ruling position in human hearts, humanity would reap immense benefits.

In the communist practice, hostility to religion clearly absorbed the Party and its functionaries far more than the task of making it redundant as a result of the socialist ideology winning the hearts of the people; no matter how quickly communism progressed, the initial plan to replace the worship of God with the worship of man in his full bloom advanced more and more into the future. So throughout its entire history, the communist system was waging its war against religion, religiosity, religious superstition, clerical obscurantism, clericalism, and particularly that despicable institution called the Catholic Church. The war was brutal, oftentimes murderous, and the atrocities committed by the communists still boggle the mind. The communists felt—quite rightly—that the Church and Christianity were the strongest barriers that protected the nation against the regime and its ideology, and that their power would not be secure until the Christians were totally subdued. In Poland, the strongly felt allegiance to the Catholic faith as well as the historically well-established position of the Catholic Church within the society were perhaps—regardless of the political games that the bishops sometimes played with the regime—the key factor that accounts for the fact that too many Poles never really sold their souls to the communist regime.

But communism, although eventually defeated, enjoyed a considerable success in various fields, also in strengthening and enlarging the antireligion front. It supplied an additional fuel to the anti-Christian, and particularly anti-Catholic streak that had long been present in the European tradition, also in Poland, even though, despite the new powerful means of propaganda, it never managed to change the overall pro-Catholic stance of the majority of the Polish population. Also in Poland, the biggest inroads made by the communists' anti-Catholic propaganda were among educated groups, especially the intellectuals who took over the old, prewar secular stereotypes and imbued them with so much venom that it paralyzed their own moral reflexes and pushed them to endorsing, without a moment's hesitation, the most outrageous acts of brutality perpetrated by the regime against the Catholics and the Church. There is a well-known letter, nowadays spoken of most reluctantly, written by a group of the leading Polish writers and intellectuals in the early 1950s condemning the Cracow priests whom the communists charged of spying for the Vatican and America; the charge was utterly nonsensical, but the sentences were ruthless. The letter is a dark page, unfortunately one of many, in the history of the intellectuals' depravity in this age of human folly. It may be that those intellectuals who were duped or duped themselves to serve totalitarianism were occasionally capable of feeling guilt for what they had done, but it seems that this infamous letter signed by Wisława Szymborska (future Nobel Prize winner in literature), Sławomir Mrożek (a prominent playwright) and others did not provoke any special moral self-examination: supporting the communists in their war against the Church must have appeared to them ideologically the least doubtful of the moral transgressions that they committed.

In communism, whoever was against religion and against Christianity made a first step to make a good comrade and to deserve special protection from the Party, but, above all, to earn a label of being enlightened. No true communist doubted that each human being with a minimal claim to intelligence had to be agnostic or atheist, that he had to be highly critical of the priests, harsh toward the Holy Scriptures, and flippant about Church dogmas, and all this was believed to be not a revolutionary eccentricity, but a continuation of the most enlightened European traditions, especially those of the Enlightenment. The Party intellectuals convinced themselves, through fear, ignorance, and self-deception, that their humiliating servility was not that, but a somewhat modernized version of Voltairianism.

Unfortunately the Christian faith did not make the believers immune to the communist temptation. For a long time there was a trend in Christianity with an obsequious proclivity toward communism and socialism, which probably sprouted out of common strong anticapitalist sentiments, but also of a conviction shared by some Christians, but not reciprocated by the secular Left, that both Christianity and socialism in their roots stemmed from the same moral impulse, the good of the people. Both Protestants and Catholics and even the greatest of theologians fell prey to this illusion. Karl Barth, Paul Tillich, Jacques Maritain, and many others had such episodes. Some, like Emmanuel Mounier, went clearly beyond sympathy and became openly pro-communist and pro-Soviet fellow travelers. Thousands of pastors and Roman Catholic and Eastern Orthodox priests joined the system and for many years served it faithfully out of stupidity, opportunism, ideological blindness, or betrayal, all of which they supported with pathetic intellectual contortions. Dean of Canterbury Hewlett Johnson was once Stalin's notorious puppet at propaganda meetings organized by the Soviet Communist Party.

In Poland, the Church was sabotaged from inside by renegade priests, whom the communist authorities called—in the mendacious language so typical of them—"patriot priests" and whose number in absolute terms was by no means small. When the terror abated and indoctrination began to subside, the communists tried another strategy, this time by luring a larger group of Catholics into the system, not only traitors and pathological opportunists. They even allowed a small Party group of Catholics to be represented in the Parliament, which, for many, seemed a promising beginning of an evolutionary change for the better. At one point, immediately after the 1956 thaw, the Polish episcopate officially urged their flock to support the reformist policies of the Communist Party, and the government gave permission to establish a few quasi-independent associations of Catholic persuasion. It soon became clear, however, that no further changes would be made and no further political plurality tolerated. But the door for those Catholics who wished to support the regime was still open.

The Communist Party went so far as to encourage what was then called a dialogue between Marxists and Catholics. To launch such a dialogue was on the one hand a propaganda ploy to show how the communists cooperated with all the people of good will, but on the other, a clever tactic to divide the Catholics and to push those intransigent into the corner. Whatever the reason of the propagandists, the mere fact that the so-called dialogue lasted for at least a decade proved that the communist ideology was still effective. Behind the decision of quite a few of those Catholic intellectuals who decided to converse with the Marxists was a sort of practical imperative. They felt that socialism/communism was inevitable, ubiquitous, and philosophically unchallengeable, and therefore thought it a matter of urgency for the Catholics within the world as it was (or, rather, as they believed it was) to find a safe place and obtain some kind of official intellectual legitimacy.

This dialogue, when we look at it today, is not an uplifting spectacle and reveals an essential asymmetry between the two sides. One had to make serious concessions to accommodate itself to the communist reality. The other conceded nothing, promised nothing, and treated its opponents patronizingly. The Catholics' concessions were the following: they spoke highly of socialism as both theory and practice and distanced themselves from those bad Catholics who did not appreciate the benefits and virtues of the new regime. They postulated that because Catholicism had much in common with socialism, the Church should be more listened to and its presence more recognized in the socialist society. The Marxists, in turn, made no concessions at all. They noted with satisfaction the fact that progressive Catholics finally came to accept socialism, although they should have done it sooner, and that they came to denounce the bad Catholics, although they should have done it more forcefully. To the Catholics' postulate the Marxists responded that of course the Catholics could find their place in the process of building socialism, but they must be aware that socialism had the higher value and that because the historical record of the Church was ugly, they should try harder than others to earn the trust of the socialist community.

The Catholic Church in Poland, led by Primate Stefan Wyszyński (later to be called the Primate of the Millennium), was generally hostile to this rapprochement. The Polish episcopate, however, had not been so adamant in the past: they had treated the "patriot priests" with surprising leniency and made declarations that were quite painful to the faithful (for example, condemning anticommunist resistance groups as "gangs"). But in his rejection of the dialogue, Primate Wyszyński was right. He did not trust the intellectuals, and in fact had never trusted them, as one can see from a well-known article published before World War II when the specter of communist Poland was not yet in sight. Hence, his decision to make the Catholicism of the people—the folk Catholicism, so to speak—the stronghold of the Catholic faith was quite understandable and compatible with his deep convictions. The decision had far-reaching and generally positive effects: by relying on rural religiosity the Church managed to preserve a large area of social practices and religious traditions that was not accessible to the communist ideology. In countries where this type of folk Christianity did not exist or was considerably weaker, the communist system managed to wreak more havoc and penetrated deeper into the social fabric.

The Primate's decision, however, had negative effects as well. Polish Catholicism survived in amazingly good shape, but not without flaws: what it clearly lacked was intellectual leadership. Most of the Catholic intelligentsia represented so-called open Catholicism, which had scarcely any influence on the people's minds and souls, or if it had, was largely destructive. Probably the only period when one could see a close alliance between the Church and the intelligentsia was in the 1980s, but the love affair was short, and its disappearance was as abrupt as its coming into being. No signs indicating that it would happen appeared before and it would have been almost incomprehensible were it not for the emergence of the magnetic personality of Karol Wojtyła, who ascended to the papal throne in 1978. Unfortunately this cordial alliance came apart even before the fall of communism. It is interesting to note that its beginning and its end were proclaimed by the same man, Adam Michnik, a top anti-regime dissident, who for decades has been dictating to the Polish herd of independent minds which way they should be going. When read today, both of his proclamations—marking the beginning and the end of the entente cordiale with the Church—disclose what previously was overlooked, namely, a consistently anti-Church and antireligious bias that has now been laid bare after the rhetoric of purely tactical concern for the fate of the Church and religion in Poland became worn out and lost its persuasive power.

Due to the absence of the vigorous Catholic intelligentsia, the effects of communism on the Polish elites proved more durable than previously thought and an antireligious ideology left a permanent mark on the soul of Polish academics, writers, and artists. No wonder, then, that after the fall of the regime an antireligious attitude, this time in a new and liberal-democratic formula, found fertile ground and spread quickly among a wide range of educated people, and even more quickly among those who, though downright stupid, had intellectual pretensions because they graduated from something or other, or, as was not uncommon, worked at some educational institution. It simply did not occur to them that the Church was so helpful to the nation under communism not because she was simply against this particular political system, but because the system was wrong in everything and the Church was right in almost all the issues that were crucial to the existence of a viable society. And if so, the Church should have been worth listening to regardless of what political arrangement the society took, and perhaps even more so after the communist regime fell and the liberal democrats took over.

★ 2 ★

The attitude of liberalism toward religion was, from the start, frosty and sometimes hostile. Like the socialists later on, the liberals were aware of the great ideological power wielded by religion (although the term "ideology" had not been coined yet), which they found politically most troubling. Religion, they said, provokes deep divisions, incites civil wars, pushes people to violence against their neighbors. The grounds for this view as well as a general philosophical framework for the classical liberal concept of religion were provided by the Reformation.

Speaking somewhat simplistically, the Protestants moved religion more than ever before into the realm of faith, so that its outward forms and even its dogmatic aspect lost their importance. They brought back St. Paul's old distinction between the inner man and the outer man, which they translated into the analogous distinction between internal and external religion; the former was considered to be appropriate and protected, the latter, secondary and not deserving of any special protection. It was the external form—the "traditions and additions," as John Milton called them—that could destabilize the political order and generate irresponsible behavior, zealousness, fanaticism, and a desire to convert dissidents by force.

The controversy that was going on at that time between the tolerationists and antitolerationists, i.e., those who wanted to allow the public presence of external religion and those who wanted to have it significantly reduced, heated though it was, did not dramatically set apart the disputing parties. Both actually agreed that internal religion deserved respect because—and both used the same argument—this is so deeply embedded in the human soul that it is impervious to any political control, including the most ruthless coercion; they also agreed that external religion can be politically dangerous and is arguably the most important source of political conflict. The major difference between the two parties was that the antitolerationists asserted that outer religion should be totally controlled by the government, while the tolerationists, such as the old John Locke (the young Locke belonged to the opposite camp), allowed for its public presence, sometimes quite considerable, but gave the state the right to supervise its religious rites and dogmas politically. If any among these rites and dogmas appeared to threaten social peace, public order, existing laws, or political stability, then—claimed Locke and others like-minded thinkers—the state should not hesitate to step in and remove the threat. Such a decision would be purely political, not religious. The government or its officials banning a rite or a dogma would not be motivated by its alleged religious truth or falsehood—such verdicts would not be in their power to make—but would solely assess its practical consequences for the stability of the political order.

The political argument was also behind the exclusion of Catholics from the shield of religious toleration, a standard rule among the Protestant tolerationists. It was claimed that the Catholics were not trustworthy as other citizens because of their divided loyalty—one part to the country, the other to Rome, whereas a good citizen could not have but one sovereign, the state. This exclusion was widely supported in the Protestant countries, apparently in the belief, considered self-evident, that whatever message a religion conveys, it cannot override the will of the sovereign and cannot exempt citizens from civic obedience. But because the genuine religion was inner religion, this prerogative that gave the state the power to supervise outer religion did not seem, to those who accepted it, particularly painful.

Regardless of how sincerely the Reformation theologians desired to liberate religion from the institutional straitjacket, and how ardently they defended the purity of faith, the overall result of the schism was different. Religion, freed from the dictates of Rome, fell under the control of the state, to which the liberals, so distrustful of revealed religion of any kind, readily assented. It is often said that the controversy over toleration led—thanks to the perseverance of the liberals—to the establishment of a constitutional principle of the separation of church and state, which was to become one of the key standards in liberal-democratic societies. Nothing could be further from the truth. This principle was binding in the United States, but certainly not in European Protestant societies. In the United States the First Amendment ruled out the existence of what it calls an established religion (which, in fact, means the state religion). What Britain and several other Protestant countries did was the opposite: by making the head of state the head of the church they instituted something that clearly falls into a category of established religion.

The idea that the state is the ultimate supervisor in all matters relating to the political community, including religious ones, had a long tradition and in itself was not revolutionary. The problem was that the state could go too far in imposing discipline and be tempted to use the argument from political rationality to extirpate some religious groups deemed suspect, to violate human conscience on a massive scale, and to usurp the role of the spiritual and moral authority under the pretext of a disinterested political supervision. That has occasionally happened in Europe for several centuries, usually at the times of political turmoil (e.g., the brutal persecution of Catholics after Henry VIII broke with Rome), or when the state officially accepted an ideological agenda hostile to Christianity (as was the case after the French Revolution when the new assembly passed the civil constitution for the clergy). The usual practice was to humiliate the potentially suspect group by forcing them to take an oath, interpreted as a purely political act of allegiance, on the regulations that they found morally repugnant or religiously unacceptable (as in the case of Thomas More, who, despite his de facto loyalty to the British monarchy, after the king's breach with Rome was executed for not having taken the oath on the Act of Supremacy).

With respect to the separation of Church and State, the Catholic countries in Europe fared better than the Protestant countries. The secular and the ecclesiastical powers were by definition separated: in Catholicism, the supreme authority in the Church was in the hands of the Pope, who was sovereign with respect to the powers of emperors, kings, and presidents. Such was, of course, the theory. In practice, the relations between Throne and Altar varied, and in a long and complicated history of these relations we have had various combinations: from the de facto subordination of one authority to another, through close cooperation, to deep political and doctrinal conflicts. Of course, some time after the religious wars in Europe ended, religious peace prevailed (with the exceptions of such extraordinary developments as the French Revolution). As the situation became stabilized, most governments in Protestant and Catholic countries pursued the policy of accommodation, not interfering too much in religious matters and thus respecting in practice religious liberties.

This began to change in recent decades when the European governments, by having espoused an ambitious ideological mission, started legislating morality in an open confrontation with the teaching of Christianity (and other religions). Moreover, to justify their policy they used an analogous political argument—spurious, as it is easy to see, but enormously effective—that ran as follows: "What we enforce is the law of the land and constitutional rights—be it in the matters of abortion, marriage, education, life, death—and not religion, and what we supervise is not the people's souls, but our citizens' loyalty to the existing legal and political system." This offensive was so formidable that a lot of religious groups, mostly Protestant, but some Catholic too, acquiesced. Those that acquiesced had to adapt their teaching to the requirements of the liberal-democratic state and, consequently, to revise their doctrines substantially, sometimes beyond recognition. Those that resisted put themselves on a collision course with the liberal-democratic state and, as their critics repeatedly said, with modernity as such.

Fideism—characteristic of Protestantism but spreading beyond its boundaries—which encouraged the subordination of external religion to the state, caused a gradual marginalization of Christianity in the public realm, which, as was to be expected, had to result in progressive secularization. In any highly political society, as a liberal society is, whatever lacks political legitimacy to appear in the public square loses its raison d'être altogether. Internal religion, regarded as the only form of religion that could be tolerated if it wanted to retain this quasi-protection, had to seek some political respectability, and the only way to do it was, first, to dispel any suspicion that it might undermine liberalism in human souls, and furthermore, to prove that it motivates people to do things that are politically useful, such as bringing about peace, preaching the attitude of toleration, and inspiring philanthropy. In other words, religion was to demonstrate that it supported the liberal order and helped the liberal state to perform its functions. Religion in a nonpolitical sense should be confined to the church and the inner life, or, better yet, exclusively to the inner life and family life because, for example, a politician ostentatiously going to church could be accused of encroaching on the secularity of the state. Those Christians who took this view did not put up a heroic fight against the liberal state usurping the role of the legislator of morality. The usurper seized his power almost unopposed, and his victorious army did not even bother to take prisoners.

★ 3 ★

Democratic theories, as opposed to liberal ones, do not emit such an obvious critical message about religion, but neither are they particularly favorable. The basic objection was that the divisions in the democratic system should be political, which meant that they should have as their foundation different ideas about how to organize the state and its institutions, and under no circumstance should they relate to religion. The political parties could be socialist, liberal, conservative, monarchist, or anarchist, but they must not be Catholic, or Evangelical, or Orthodox; nor could they be based on ethnicity or race. The democratic state should provide a place for different ethnic groups, different races, or different religions, but it could not endorse one race or religion at the expense of others. A democratic man is a citizen of the state, and citizenship does not differentiate between races, ethnic groups, or religions. The difference between the so-called mature democratic societies and those societies that not have reached political maturity (whatever the exact meaning of it may be) is precisely that in the latter, people are not grouped around political parties, but around tribes, clans, and religious cults.

This core of this argument is correct, but its general formulation can be misleading. In the course of the intellectual and political history of Europe, Christian religion did influence—and significantly so—political programs, including concepts of the state, the duties of the citizen, and the hierarchy of political objectives. Thus one can legitimately speak of Christian political thought developing since the Middle Ages to modern times, rich in content and diverse in implications. It is therefore obvious that political parties may be and in fact have been called Christian, although it is also true that no specific, single political system doctrine can be derived from Christian philosophical and theological heritage.

Removing Christianity from the public square, be it directly or indirectly, was a decision taken not only against religion as such, and against this particular religion, but against certain political ideas having a long and honorable tradition, which could have had a positive effect on the institutional order and on our thinking about politics. Of course, the primary impulse of the critics was a strong anti-Christian bias, not a rational desire to save politics from what did not properly belong to it. In liberalism as it emerged in early modernity there were additional factors, such as a vehement rejection of medieval philosophy and of scholastics in particular, with which Christianity was often associated. Sometimes the modern philosophers, hostile to Christianity and to the Catholic Church as they were, had an ambitious plan to find an entirely new theological basis for the political order, with no reference to previous theories or the classical tradition. Authors such as Hobbes and Locke, nominally Christian, sought a new interpretation of the Christian religion, this time with no links to existing tradition (which made them, of course, automatically anti-Catholic), but congruent with the modern view of the rationality they recognized. The religion thus transformed and radically diluted was said to be free from alleged anachronisms and made palatable to the tastes and needs of modern man. Hobbes devoted half of his *Leviathan* to religion, where, while not directly denying Christianity, he interpreted it in the way modern man, without the burden of scholastic philosophy and armed with the achievements of new natural sciences, could accept. Hobbes told him what hell and heaven could be in light of reason, and which parts of Christian teaching were defensible and which were not. Locke's approach was similar. In his *The Reasonableness of Christianity* he explained how a man having Locke's view on politics and knowledge should interpret basic teachings of the Christian religion with the intention to save it for modern times.

Such theoretical exercises were meant to liberate people from the irrationality within which they remained enslaved, having believed in religions, superstitions, revelations, miracles, magical rites to purify their souls, and fantastic stories about the afterlife. All this entangled those thinkers in a paradox—typical of modern thinking—intermingling coercion with liberation. Because religion was believed to have pushed man to the phantasmagorias invented by unthinking minds and by authoritarian institutions such as the Church, the subjection of people to political coercion was not only an act of liberating them from the yoke of ignorance and servitude, but also of strengthening their freedom. The political coercion was rational insofar as it limited itself to self-evident goals, such as peace and cooperation, which should clearly be considered as a most natural expectation of every living creature. This is the reason why John Locke the liberal could, without contradicting himself, preach religious toleration while granting the state vast prerogatives to control religious practices and ideas, and to use coercion if these put at risk political peace and social cooperation.

Kant made a similar point in his famous essay on the Enlightenment. He started with the triumphant announcement that the human race had left the stage of adolescence, which for him meant a very precise thing, namely that man had freed himself from the influence of religion and was at last able to use his reason as the sovereign authority. Kant concluded his essay by praising the autocratic rule of Frederick the Great as a great victory of freedom. The same argument, albeit in a cartoonish form, is found in Voltaire, who in his work on toleration was depicting with a predictably obsessive monotony what he thought to be the persistently harmful influence of Christianity on every society and epoch; while bashing Christians he shamelessly justified various autocrats and tyrants in the history of Europe and Asia. He commended, for example, the Romans for their repression of Christians—in which he saw an act of toleration—and criticized the repressed Christians who, as he said, provoked the Romans with their intolerant religious zeal.

The most radical version of making religion a servant of politics we owe to Jean-Jacques Rousseau, notably in his concept of "civil religion," which was intended as the bedrock of the deep emotional cohesion in a society. This new type of religious belief was to supersede the earlier forms, of which he enumerated three: a religion exclusively internal, a religion of traditional societies based on social mores and rituals, and a religion most bizarre, which for him was Christianity, primarily Catholic, but partly Protestant too. What was bizarre about it was its being both otherworldly and this-worldly, the combination of which was politically pernicious, because it undermined the unity of a community and subverted the sovereign power of the state. The new religion he proposed was an artificial construction invented solely to serve a political purpose, but it contained elements from other religions (the existence of a powerful and compassionate deity, the sanctity of law, and the belief in the afterlife, where the righteous are rewarded and the wicked punished). The function of the civil religion resembled that of an ideology—giving a society deprived of old loyalties a new identity and a new sense of belonging. The imposition of the civil religion was primarily a political operation with implications similar to those that were later to be seen in highly ideological regimes: the sovereign could get rid of nonbelievers and even punish with death those who betrayed the new religious dogmas.

The anti-Catholic and anti-Church attitude was something that from the beginning permeated the liberal notion of politics. Because the majority of the liberal thinkers were or were born Protestants, the antidespotic edge of their theory found in the Catholic Church an obvious villain. Their religious background and their theories reinforced each other. With the monarchies weakening or turning into constitutional parliamentary systems, the Church and her religion remained unabashedly and ostentatiously at the nonliberal position, as if deliberately provoking all liberal critics to use all the polemical artillery.

Nineteenth-century socialism, with its hostility to religion, is in a way a version of a similar attitude—the Church and Catholicism represented an old order that long ago outlived its usefulness and deserved to perish. The twentieth-century version was, of course, rhetorically and in practice far more deadly. The architects and helmsmen of the communist system were convinced that when fighting religion, whatever the means, they did humanity a great service by contributing to its liberation: the more radical the coercive means applied, the nearer they thought was the time when man became his own master. The fact that the antireligion policies of the communists were so much more brutal than those of the liberal and democratic states is, of course, crucial and should never be forgotten or minimized, but it remains true that their views on religion, and on Christianity in particular, converged too often. When in the early 1920s Bertrand Russell, after having visited Bolshevik Russia, wrote a book on the theory and practice of Bolshevism, he in no uncertain words expressed both his admiration for the general idea of the system, and his equally strong distaste for the means used. He finished his book on the relatively optimistic note that the communist program, once freed from the Asianlike barbaric heritage so powerfully present in Russia, would remain a great hope of mankind.

The communists were indeed aware that such were the feelings of the liberal-minded Western elites, and, wishing to ease the criticism of their brutal policies, willingly presented themselves as continuing the Western secular and anti-Christian tradition. This tactic proved quite effective, as it gave the communists an image of splendidly daring modernizers. After all, both the communists and the Western liberal progressives shared an assumption that religion, unless itself radically modernized, was an impediment to modernization; both shared a similar vision of a better world to come in which there would be no religion at all, or, if it was to survive, it would be entirely subservient to the ideas and institutions of the new society. Neither the communists nor liberal progressives could ever imagine religion to be a carrier of wisdom and a valuable corrective force that was necessary to challenge the dogmas of the grand plan of modernization. To accept its authority, if only partially, would have been as unthinkable to them as it would have been for Kant to argue that man, after having matured, should go back to the state of adolescence.

This notion that to be for freedom and modernity presumes being also anti-Christian has imprinted itself on the European mind and is as strong today as it was in the past. An anti-Christian rhetoric in the media and in politics and anti-Christian art, including paintings, installations, plays, novels, films, articles, and slogans, fills the public space today, making the Christian religion, its institutions, and its articles of faith objects of endlessly multiplying derisions and accusations. Homosexual activists see Christianity as the original source of homophobia and feminists as the foundation of patriarchy. Countless intellectuals accuse it of totalitarianism, reactionary sexual ethics, pedophilia, an Inquisition-like mentality, witch-hunts, anti-Semitism and the Holocaust, intellectual infantilism, a morbid fascination with guilt, and numerous other sins. On the one hand, there is an ever-present feeling of satisfaction that Christianity has been in retreat for some time, being driven back by a victorious wave of secularization; on the other, it is invariably seen as an evil that miraculously resurrects itself and continues to cast its ominous shadow over Western civilization. The participation of Christians in public life—even as paltry as it is now—revives the usual suspicions and resuscitates the old anti-Christian stereotypes. The crusade against Christianity verges on the absurd: liberals continue to make new conquests and to colonize more and more areas of human life, leaving practically no territory outside their control, and the more they grab, the louder they rant against Christianity, flogging it with new accusations, invectives, and blasphemies.

The analogy to what was happening under the communist rule seems irresistible. In the countries where, as a result of brutal repressions by the Communist regime, sometimes induced by historical and cultural peculiarities, Christianity was believed to be on the wane, and where the forces of secularism triumphed to the satisfaction of the apostles of the communist ideology, the anti-Christian warriors did not lay down their arms: they continued to fight, as if fearing that Christianity's death was temporary and that the religion, reborn again, was soon to resume its sinister role as a major obstacle to the march of modernity. In a sense, the communists were right: much of the resistance that finally led to the disintegration of the communist system came from religious groups and from religion itself. At the end of the day it turned out that the fear of religion was justified: the Pope had indeed far more troops than the communist dictators. It is quite possible that the anti-Christian crusaders of today are haunted by a similar fear.

In today's liberal democracy the anti-Christian attitude has been slightly modified. An authoritarian rhetoric, willingly used in the past by even the most renowned tolerationists, such as Locke and Bayle, disappeared. The public space, including public language, has been for some time governed by two formal rules. These rules, long present in liberal thinking, are now included in the legal and constitutional systems and are believed to have settled once and for all the problem of religion and politics. First, religious freedom is recognized as a fundamental human right, and second, the state must be ideologically neutral. In real terms, the first rule entails that no religious group can be prevented from practicing their religion; the second asserts that the state must be free from any religion and is not allowed to support any. Theoretically, the solution is clear, but despite appearances, the old problems did not vanish. The allegedly formal rules turned out to be substantive.

First of all, what these rules legitimized was an assumption that Christianity should be treated like other religions, and that there was no reason why it should have a superior status. Such an assumption would have been inconceivable to most of the old tolerationists; even Voltaire, clearly loathing Christianity, explicitly rejected this view in his *Treatise on Toleration*, admitting that the position of this religion in Europe was exceptional and therefore privileged. The new rules were, in the intentions of the liberals, universalist, and thus allowed no exceptions either on historical or philosophical grounds. This universalism the liberals were particularly proud of, because they saw in it a manifestation of their neutrality. They, however, disregarded an obvious fact that in practice what they called neutrality has irrevocably dethroned Christianity from the position it had had for many centuries and thus led to redefining the nature of European civilization.

As one can see, the rules in question, although intended to be formal, were easily adapted to the prevailing ideology and soon became a part of it. Today they are among the standard inventory of those who assume the irrelevance of Christianity for the identity of Western civilization or, stating it more mildly, who assume the post-Christian nature of this civilization in which Christianity is a fortunately closed chapter.

The view that the modern world is essentially non-Christian, only timidly uttered a few decades ago, is now widely accepted. Articulated explicitly and loudly by philosophers, political scientists, and writers, it has penetrated public opinion and become a sort of uncontested axiom of social wisdom. A reference to Christianity as an important part of European identity in the Preamble to the EU Constitutional Treaty provoked such an angry reaction that it had to be dropped as allegedly incongruent with what the EU calls "European values." Even acknowledging the historical role of the Christian heritage is now thought too extravagant to be tolerated. All these manifestations of an anti-Christian sentiment are not a trifling matter. They illustrate the triumph of the ideological thinking whose distinguishing feature is a reorganization, and quite often a falsification, of the past in order to put it at the service of the contemporary political project. "Who controls the past controls the future," as Orwell accurately observed in his dissection of totalitarianism. The communists did it on a large scale; the EU in its effort to build a new European identity is doing something quite similar, though on a smaller scale.

Paralyzed by their Christophobia (to use Joseph H. H. Weiler's well-known expression), the European Union as well as the European governments do not react to the brutal persecution of Christians in other continents, and if they do, their reaction is low-key. This is all the more shameful that the Christians are—and it must be repeated over and over again—the most persecuted religious group in the world. It seems almost unthinkable that the EU of today would take a more resolute stand by, for instance, asserting that due to the special role of Christianity in the history of Europe, Europeans have an obligation to defend the Catholics, Protestants, and Christians of other denominations in other continents who are imprisoned, expelled, tortured, and massacred. More outspoken statements condemning the persecution are rare and written in a universalist language in which the Christians are mentioned alongside other groups, as if the EU were afraid to be too committal. It is significant that in the famous case of *Lautsi v. Italy*, where the first verdict by the European Court of Human Rights decided that crucifixes in schools were unacceptable, most other European governments did not support the Italian government, which appealed the ruling, and failed to act as amicus curiae. Those that did—Armenia, Bulgaria, Cyprus, Greece, Lithuania, Malta, Monaco, Romania, Russia, and San Marino—were either secondary players within the EU, or, like Russia, outside it. None of the major European countries sided with the Italians. Neither did, I am ashamed to say, Poland under the Civic Platform government. The Polish government, sensitive to what the big guys might think about it, decided not to get involved.

This coldness to the plight of Christians and Christianity is concealed by the language of universalistic egalitarianism which in its ostentatious generosity is supposed to express concern for all religions and all religious groups. But the principle of equality and its two rules—equal freedom of all religions and neutrality of the state—are anything but generous. Under the banner of equality the religion that has been of paramount importance is being equalized with the religions that had no importance at all. In concrete terms the equalization means that Christianity must be drastically devalued while other religions of little impact on European identity are given a tremendous boost.

The nonsense of this new perspective leaps to the eye. For example, some of the British bishops and politicians played with an idea of introducing elements of sharia law into the British legal system in areas with a large Muslim population so that the Muslims could feel better in a Christian environment; those who came with this generous offer seemed to forget that British society has already effectively eliminated Christianity, and what they suggested would amount to making Britain more Muslim, while pushing Christianity further aside. Another example is the law prohibiting the wearing of religious symbols: while it originally targeted Muslims, it has in fact become a major legal measure to eliminate from the public presence the Christian symbols that for two millennia have been an integral part of Western civilization.

Such actions are reminiscent of the wars against religious symbols waged by the communist government against religious communities on the pretext that these symbols violated the secular character of state institutions. The communist authorities did not tolerate crucifixes in schools and were irritated when the citizens of the communist state were wearing them in a too-conspicuous manner. If the judgment of the European Court of Human Rights in the case of *Lautsi v. Italy* had been upheld in the Grand Chamber, the Italian schools (and in the end probably also the schools in other countries) would have been similar to those in the communist countries, where the presence of crosses in classrooms or holy medals around the necks of students would be extirpated by law. In the first case, the censure would have been enforced by the European Court of Human Rights, and in the other, by the system of communist justice, but the practical consequences for the Christians would have been the same. It is also worth remembering that most communist countries—after the brutal attempts to annihilate religion had failed—also upheld the two rules of freedom of religious worship and the ideological neutrality of the state. The communists were perfectly happy to accept these rules as long as they meant that religious communities were not allowed to make nonreligious public statements other than those that supported the regime. The Polish communist authorities also willingly resorted to those rules whenever they thought it expedient to reduce the significance of Catholicism; then they took the pose of a neutral arbiter and in the name of what they called fairness gave a disproportionately well-publicized hearing to various representatives of small churches, particularly those that were unconditionally endorsing the Communist Party, having been sometimes infiltrated by the Secret Police, and were eager to take part in any anti-Catholic action.

The decision about the public presence of religion based on the two mentioned rules is—let me reiterate—to a large degree substantive, not formal, and the substance depends on the ideological interpretation given to it by the governing bodies. In themselves these principles do not determine much but the intention of the interpreters pushes them in one direction or another and gives them a substantive character. The rules, stated out of any context, include too many components vague or unsaid: freedom of religion is never absolute, religious communities never limit themselves to religious matters, the state is never neutral and has its own ideological preferences, etc. Under communism, the government hated religion and used both rules to eliminate Christianity from the public square and, ultimately, from the people's hearts and minds. The Communist Constitution, of course, guaranteed equality of religions and religious freedom; there was an article added to it stipulating that this freedom must not be used to attack the socialist system. The article was completely superfluous: with or without it the policy of the Communist Party toward the Church and the Catholics would have been the same. When read in the context of the liberal-democratic rules, the article did not say anything shocking: liberal democracy takes for granted that the churches do not attack the political system in which they live: that is, the system of liberal democracy. If they do, they are in trouble.

In the United States—that is, in a country where one could speak of the real separation of church and state—the power, at least until the 1960s, was in the hands of the Christian majority, mostly Protestant, who interpreted the rules of freedom of religion and neutrality of the state in a way that allowed for a strong presence of religion in the public square, to the extent that American society could be accurately called the society of the Book. In today's postcommunist Poland, Catholicism has been the subject of constant attacks since the moment the old regime collapsed, but the Church still retains an important position in the life of the country, which comes not from constitutional provisions but her political and historical role in the nation's history and the existence of a large Catholic community. In today's Europe, the power has been in the hands of the political class hostile to Christianity, and this class, supported by the elites and by large segments of society, has been interpreting the two rules—with complete impunity—in a manner appropriate to its anti-Christian prejudice.

Hostility to Christianity in modern liberal democracies raises the question of how religion should manifest itself in public life.

The simplest answer—close to what some Protestant movements embodied—is that religious life and political life should be separated. Religion is essentially a private matter, a family matter, and sometimes a community matter, but definitely not a state matter. There are quite a lot of people today who are public figures, professionals, politicians, and it is rarely that we know what religion, if any, they profess, and even if we knew, this would be irrelevant in the assessment of their public performance. Such a strict separation of the religious and the public realms is very much in tune with today's ideology of modernity. And it is all the more convincing that it confirms the assumption—considered obvious but, in fact, doubtful—that the freedom of religion is guaranteed in Western democracies, and that Christians, being denied a public presence, should have no reason to complain.

This strategy—let us call it conciliatory—should be distinguished from another one—let us call it capitulatory. The difference between the first and the second is at the beginning one of degree, but ultimately one of essence. The aim of the conciliatory Christians has been to avoid conflicts with the liberal democrats and to adapt themselves to the existing system, which they thought sufficiently spacious and friendly to include Christianity together with other religions; the aim of the Christians who have capitulated is to be admitted to the liberal-democratic club, and in order to do it they are willing to accept any terms and concessions, convinced that remaining outside this club or being refused entrance would bring infamy on them.

One can, of course, defend both strategies, conciliation and capitulation, and the standard argument of defense is the following: an enormous part of the activities of churches and an enormous area of religion have nothing to do with politics, socialism, liberal democracy, or anything related. Religion and churches are about God, souls, and salvation. Therefore, because we live in a civil society governed by the rule of law, waging big political battles against it is not only meaningless from the perspective of religion but pulls the churches away from their primary mission, which is that of evangelization.

No doubt the basic objectives of Christianity remain outside politics, and it is these objectives that the churches and the faithful should pursue. But this otherwise obvious statement fails to address one crucial fact: the growing infiltration of liberal democracy into religion. Liberal democracy, like socialism, has an overwhelming tendency to politicize and ideologize social life in all its aspects, including those that were once considered private; hence, it is difficult for religion to find a place in a society where it would be free from the pressure from liberal-democratic orthodoxy and where it would not risk a conflict with its commissars. Even the issues generally thought to be remote from politics become censured by the punctilious scrutiny of those who watch over ideological purity. To give an example: the Vatican declaration *Dominus Iesus* sparked anger in many groups—more among secular and even atheist than Protestant and Orthodox—and the direct cause was the following sentence: "Therefore, there exists a single Church of Christ, which subsists in the Catholic Church, governed by the Successor of Peter and by the Bishops in communion with him" (Chapter IV, clause 17). Those who protested claimed to defend the non-Catholics who presumably could not—in light of the Declaration—achieve salvation, and thereby had their eschatological status unfairly diminished in relation to the Catholics. Why the atheists were so indignant about the fact that they would not achieve salvation, in which they did not believe, through God, whose existence they denied, can be explained only as a case of a total subjugation of the mind by politics and ideology: they did not see salvation as a theological problem but as the Catholic Church's political instrument, cleverly camouflaged by theological rhetoric, to justify her domination over other religious and nonreligious groups. In addition, the sentence in question offended their egalitarian sensibility: salvation, like anything people desire that is not recognized as a human right and distributed equally, must have appeared to them ideologically suspect.

The Church is bound to get into permanent conflicts with liberal democracy in matters of morality, which this system has appropriated and subjected to the power of legislative bodies and the courts. Today it is the legislators and the judges who decide what is and is not permitted, what is right and what is wrong, what is good and what is evil in matters of life and death. Until recently, the family ethics was to a large degree shaped—and with good results—by the Christians who continued and developed the teachings of the classical thinkers. But during the last decades this ethics was taken away from them and incorporated into the liberal-democratic mechanism. Dozens of legal decisions were taken

directly affecting family and even sexual life, and those decisions, bla-
tantly diverging from Christian teachings—for example, about abortion,
homosexuality, euthanasia—became law. Christians were forced to accept
the humiliating subordination to a law they thought immoral but whose
disobedience is penalized. Quite often, the grounds for these decisions
have strong anti-Christian overtones: Christian arguments are dismissed
as merely "religious" with the implication that as such they are irrational,
parochial, anachronistic, and unrepresentative. In many countries the
conscience clauses protecting Christians were either scrapped or made
invalid by the courts.

There is virtually no area in which the influence of Christianity has
not been challenged. Everything that Christianity imbued with its spirit,
legacy, and wisdom—education, morality, sensibility, human conduct,
even diet—the liberal-democratic order put to question and in many
cases eliminated. Sunday has become a day off from work, not a holy day.
Organized actions have been taking place—so far successfully—to lift the
ban, still existing in a few regions in Europe, on public disco events on
Good Friday. Ash Wednesday is no longer honored and the Christmas
season has become a commercial paradise, while Christmas Eve with
friends over a beer is more and more encouraged as something chic. The
laws and mindsets have been restructured in such a way that no custom
or rule having its root in Christianity can withstand the onslaught of
liberal democracy.

If the old communists lived long enough to see the world of today,
they would be devastated by the contrast between how little they themselves had managed to achieve in their antireligious war and how successful the liberal democrats have been. All the objectives the communists
set for themselves, and which they pursued with savage brutality, were
achieved by the liberal democrats who, almost without any effort and
simply by allowing people to drift along with the flow of modernity, succeeded in converting churches into museums, restaurants, and public
buildings, secularizing entire societies, making secularism the militant
ideology, pushing religion to the sidelines, pressing the clergy into docil-
ity, and inspiring powerful mass culture with a strong antireligious bias
in which a priest must be either a liberal challenging the Church or
a disgusting villain. Is not—one may wonder—this nonreligious and
antireligious reality of today's Western world very close to the vision of

the future without religion that the communists were so excited about, and which despite the millions of human lives sacrificed on the altar of progress, failed to materialize?

The triumph of anti-Christianity seems to favor the conciliatory strategy. A lot of Christian communities overpowered by the march of time gave up any idea of a head-on confrontation with liberal democracy, or even of any energetic defense policy. Those that capitulated unconditionally had to perform theological acrobatics to justify their position, and in so doing, agreed to suppress any formative ambitions of their own and remained silent when before their eyes the Christian practices and ideas were being destroyed. After making some timid gestures of resistance at the beginning, they soon agreed to recognize so-called homosexual marriage, to condone abortion, or even to tolerate euthanasia. The ubiquity of liberal-democratic rights and ethical permissiveness may have generated, in a lot of Christians, such a feeling of resignation that any vigorous resistance must have seemed to them futile. The only option left for Christians to maintain some respectability in a new world was to join the great progressive camp so that occasionally they would have an opportunity to smuggle in something that could pass for a religious message.

But this conciliatory attitude on the part of Christians is certainly wrong if it is motivated by the conviction that the current hostility to religion is a result of a misunderstanding, social contingencies, unfortunate errors committed by the Christians, or some minor ailments of modern society. The truth is that all these phenomena, as well as other anti-Christian developments, are the genuine consequences of the spirit of modernity on which the liberal democracy was founded. Modernity and anti-Christianity cannot be separated because they stem from the same root and since the beginning have been intertwined. There is nothing and has never been anything in this branch of the European tradition that would make it favorably predisposed to Christianity. The waves of hostility appeared and disappeared, ranging from outward aggression to indifference mixed with contempt, but never did the tide turn into an open and sincere sympathy. There have been several Christian authors of liberal persuasion who tried to find common elements between Christianity and liberalism, which occasionally produced interesting theoretical insights, but generally the inexorable tendency to liberalize and democratize the world that we have witnessed over the last centuries always supported the forces of anti-Christianity.

Therefore, whoever advocates the conciliatory strategy today fails or refuses to see the conditions in which Christians have been living. It is utterly mistaken to take the position that many do: namely that the Church should take over some liberal-democratic ingredients, open up to modern ideas and preferences, and then, after having modernized herself, manage to overcome hostility and reach people with Christian teachings. One can see why this plan has gained considerable popularity, but whatever its merits, it cannot succeed. During the Second Vatican Council and in the years that followed it, some Christians chose a similar path to be in tune, at least externally, with the liberal-democratic sensibilities so that the enmity would become less acute and the anti-Christian trend be reversed.

The idea of *aggiornamento* was far from self-evident and a lot of contradictory theories and strategies were put into it. But the long-term effects, whether intended or not, were quite clear. The church architecture became community-centered rather than monarchical; liturgy was simplified so as not to be too absorbing to a modern man who has less and less time for religion; Latin, incomprehensible and unpleasantly elitist, was replaced with the vernacular languages that everybody could understand; the priests ceased to behave, during the mass, like leaders and commanders, and turned *versus populum* to make an impression of being an equal among equals. All these changes, however, did not blunt the anti-Christian prejudices that the liberal-democratic spirit had been feeding on, nor did they entice more people to enter the Church to strengthen the already-decimated army of the faithful. The good things that were expected to happen did not happen. They did not—let me say it again—because they could not. An aversion to Christianity runs so deep in the culture of modernity that no blandishment or fawning on the part of the Church can change it. Going too far along this road actually threatens the very essence of Christianity. Since the Second Vatican Council, the tendency to obsequiousness has been increasing rather than diminishing, also in Poland, despite the fact that the liberal democrats never made any conciliatory gestures and their demands, paradoxically, became more peremptory.

The Catholic Church—it must be clearly emphasized—is more aware of the danger than other Christian communities. However, the priests and the bishops have been subjected to tremendous pressure, especially in Western Europe and America, to ingratiate with the liberal-democratic orthodoxy, and this pressure has sometimes been quite effective. The Vatican ruled by John Paul II and Benedict XVI was outspoken in its fidelity to the fundamental teachings of the Church, but it is difficult to predict in which direction their successors will go. Many fear that the next generation of cardinals may be more willing to compromise, especially as the fringe groups of the clergy loudly declare their readiness to flow with the liberal-democratic current. This may lure them into falling again, only deeper this time, into the same erroneous belief that an affable demeanor will silence the enemies of Christianity and propel the new hosts of the faithful to a liberalized and democratized Church.

But hostility will not subside and the new hosts of the faithful will not show up because the mechanism of de-Christianization has its own dynamics that the concessions of the Christians strengthen rather than weaken. If the Vatican Council progressives were to be presented with what the liberal democrats of today demand that the Church should do, they would be shattered. An unceasing relentless offensive to appropriate the entirety of our existence has made us complacently amenable to things that are otherwise outrageous. In order for the Church to be praised, or even to be spared the heaviest blows, it is no longer enough to make the sacral architecture less hierarchical, and more democratic, or have the priest face the faithful during the mass, or to consider the abolition of celibacy. Nowadays one must go much further: prohibit the condemnation of anything other than what the liberal-democratic orthodoxy mandates to condemn, and decree to praise everything that this orthodoxy mandates to praise. Today the Christians' devotion—or rather, surrender—to liberal democracy is measured by their enthusiastic support of the claims of homosexual activists and by the acceptance of what the feminists call women's reproductive rights. One shudders at the thought what will be expected of the Christians in a few years' time.

All this explains why the representatives of so-called open Catholicism do a disservice to the cause of Christian religion. Their relationship with liberal democracy is reminiscent of the dialogue their older colleagues conducted with Marxism. Open Catholics effusively eulogize the political system and its ideology, categorically distance themselves from closed and nonliberal Catholics, apparently in the hope that while cooperating creatively with the system they will have an opportunity to put a few droplets of Catholicism into the liberal-democratic vessels. Their interlocutors welcome this commitment to liberal democracy with satisfaction and emphatically approve of the great divide between the good Catholics and the bad Catholics (but are never tired of repeating that the divide should be deeper and should result in a sort of *cordon sanitaire* around the bad breed). They make it clear, however, that although the initiative of the few progressive dissidents is not negligible, Christianity itself is of little worth, and whatever is of value in it, it is better expressed and more forcefully implemented by liberal democracy. Not surprisingly, the open Catholics who decide to play this game have not gained much, but instead, have been subjected to an endless series of humiliations to which they have grown so accustomed that they treat them as the natural order of things. With each new move against Christianity—be it in vitro fertilization, so-called reproductive rights, or a rehabilitation of a new sexual disorder—they are the first to defend it, cheerfully arguing that, in fact, nothing harmful has happened, that it is the Catholic fundamentalists who are the guilty parties, and that after the liberal democrats give the world a new push forward, things are in much better shape than before. Cardinal Wyszyński, being under an enormous pressure, was yielding to communists, but finally said, *Non possumus*. Looking at the open Catholics, it is hard to imagine that they would ever be able to utter such words, let alone think about them, no matter how far liberal democracy pushes its anti-Christian campaign. One should rather think of the open Catholics as a group of cheerleaders with funny pom-poms, similar to those that one can see at games in America, encouraging their favorites to fight for progress.

The sad spectacle of what is most misleadingly called "dialogue" shows, as it did in the case of the Christians conversing with the Marxists several decades ago, a dramatic asymmetry—both in power and in ideology—between the two sides. In terms of power, the liberal democrats have, practically, a monopoly: they control the legislation, directly or indirectly influence court rulings, and have a powerful hold on public opinion. The Catholics are on the far margin: the most they can do is to beg favors from the rulers of today's world—provided those rulers happen to be in a good mood—but do not participate in its formation. They can only supplicate, and their supplications must not be expressed in their own language but in the language of those who hold power. They ask for acceptance of Catholicism not as Catholics but as a group whose creed does not threaten liberal democracy and can even—once they present their case with sufficient skill and credibility—be considered as supportive of it. While submitting these supplications, they are occasionally graded well by the powers that be, but no matter how these good grades increase their self-esteem, they usually lose sight of the essence of the general conflict; they mistake the favors bestowed on them every now and then with the actual position of Christianity in the world. They do not understand that the relationship between the two is inversely proportional: that the more favors are granted to the open Catholics, the weaker the position of Catholicism (or of Christianity in general) becomes.

★ 6 ★

One can look at Christianity in the modern world, and in Europe in particular, from the vantage point of an insider or an outsider. The first is a Christian to whom the presence of religion in the modern world is vitally important. He interprets—and with good reason—the war against Christianity as a process through which the West has been moving away from religion in the proper sense of the word toward some form of civil religion—the type that Rousseau wrote about—supplemented with a few new ingredients. He fears that this new creed will turn into an idolatry of the existing political system and its ideology, the creed according to which the ultimate criterion of being a good Christian will be the enthusiasm with which one welcomes the progress of liberal democracy in politics and ideology, and the readiness with which one gives Christian legitimacy to the new acts of capitulation.

These fears, alas, are not unfounded. For instance, it has become a common practice that papal teachings, as well as other fundamental documents of Christianity, are being assessed in light of the liberal-democratic ideology, as if this was the highest tribunal whose verdicts the Catholics must humbly respect. A case in point is the reception of the *Centesimus Annus*, John Paul II's important encyclical, which has been praised or criticized from exactly the same perspective, which is its attitude to democracy. Some praised the Pope for having spoken up in favor of democracy and of the free market, while others rebuked him for having been not sufficiently committed to democracy and the market economy. The former praised him as a good democrat while the latter undermined his democratic and free-market credibility. That such an evaluation of the Pope's words is seriously flawed is beyond the comprehension of modern man. Fewer and fewer people take seriously the notion that there may be some other criteria of assessment, not necessarily liberal-democratic and more important than these, and that perhaps it is in light of, as well as in the humble respect of these criteria that the liberal democrats should look critically at their own presuppositions and at the political system they have been thoughtlessly defending.

All Christians who believe that the liberal-democratic ideology is like an ordinary coat, no different from any other, that they can put on to be able to move around more easily and comfortably but inside which they will still remain the same Christians, make a mistake—and a double one to boot. The first mistake is a wrong choice of strategy. The liberal-democracy ideology uses—no matter that it does so fraudulently—the rhetoric of multiculturalism, which is supposed to give justice to the existence of different "cultures," which, precisely because they are different, are said to contribute to the richness and diversity of society. But if this were true, then Christians should compete with others for a visible presence and for influence—after all, this is what the coexistence of different groups in a liberal democracy should amount to—and in order to be a successful competitor they should act as an energetic and full blooded group, strongly committed to their cause, openly determined to imprint their mark on the world. The opposite strategy—obliterating the boundaries, diluting their message in liberal jargon, cajoling the idols of modernity, paying homage to today's superstitions, self-effacing their identity—condemns Christians to a sad defeat with no dignity and no progeny.

The second mistake is to ignore the fact that the liberal-democratic ideology has long since ceased to be open (if it ever was) and has entered a stage of rigid dogmatization. The more conquests it makes, the less the victors are willing to show clemency to anyone outside the winning forces. The Christians who put on humble faces and declare their readiness to seek a common ground of action for a better world stand no chance to survive, regardless of how far in their self-repudiation they go. Sooner or later they will have to sign an unconditional surrender and to join the system with no opt-out and no conscience clauses, or, in the event of a sudden declaration of *non possumus*, they will be instantly degraded to the position of a contemptible enemy of liberal democracy. So far, nothing indicates that the regime will lose its ideological momentum.

But the fate of Christianity in a liberal democracy can also be viewed from an external, non-Christian perspective. Those who are not Christians and, as sometimes happens, do not like Christianity, can feel Schadenfreude looking at the problems this religion encounters in the modern world, particularly a disturbing rapidity of secularization. However, such a reaction is shortsighted. Christianity is not just a religion, but a vital spiritual element of Western identity, something that allowed Europe to maintain a strong sense of continuity, linking the ancient with the modern and absorbing into itself a variety of intellectual inspirations. By rejecting Christianity—after having marginalized the classical heritage—Europe, and indeed, the entire West not only slides into cultural aridity, a process noticeable for some time, but also falls under the smothering monopoly of one ideology whose uniformity is being cleverly concealed by the deafening rhetoric of diversity that has been pouring into people's minds at all occasions and in all contexts.

Christianity is the last great force that offers a viable alternative to the tediousness of liberal-democratic anthropology. In this respect it is closer to the classical rather than the modern view of human nature. With Christianity being driven out of the main tract, the liberal-democratic man—unchallenged and totally secure in his rule—will become a sole master of today's imagination, apodictically determining the boundaries of human nature and, at the very outset, disavowing everything that dares to reach beyond his narrow perspective. The only thing he will be capable of doing is occasional, albeit capricious generosity in tolerating some form of dissidence at the far peripheries of his empire. Without a strong competitor the liberal-democratic man will reign over human aspirations like a tyrant. There will appear no one who would dare or be ready, in compliance with the existing rules, to call his reign into question; the rules that exist do not permit such extravagant acts, and a supposition that there might be other rules has long since been discarded as absurd.

One can, of course, imagine that the liberal-democratic monopoly will eventually begin to crack and that new centrifugal forces, from causes yet unfathomed, will be set in motion. Common sense and experience tell us that it is not possible for people to be lulled by one ideology forever and to have their emotions and thoughts organized always in the same way. The war against the Christian heritage, however, may have this unpleasant consequence: when the renewal comes, it will start from a much lower level than the one reached previously by European culture through Christianity. Liberal-democratic man, in order to shake out his habits, superstitions, prejudices, dogmas, self-mystification, hypocrisy, and many other faults, inborn as well as those acquired through a prolonged period of monopolist rule, will have before him a much harder road than did the previous rulers of the human imagination. He is more stubborn, more narrow-minded, and clearly less willing to learn from others. The rediscovery of the Revelation, after denigrating that part of human nature that allowed its prior acceptance, will require new stimuli and a new surge of spiritual energy, of which we cannot, in the time of growing secularization, say anything definite, or even whether they will be at all possible.

CONCLUSION

One can look at the affinities between communism and liberal democracy from both a narrow and a wider prospect. The narrower point of view may lead us to a sad conclusion that the modern Western world never really understood the communist experience quite correctly and if it did, it never took seriously the lessons that followed from it. When looked at more broadly, the examination of those affinities may give grounds for a conclusion more daring: namely, that the two regimes stem from the same root, or more precisely, from the same, not particularly good, inclination of modern man, persistently revealing itself under different political circumstances. This is assuredly not the only disquieting inclination that modern man has given in to, bearing in mind the bloody history of Europe and America in the last centuries. But the story of the relationship between communism and liberal democracy is of particular importance, as it is about the systems that were hailed and sincerely believed to be the greatest hopes of mankind. The story is thus not only about politics, but also, indirectly, about the aspirations and dreams of modern man.

This book argued that the modern man who was the inspiring force of the two political systems was a mediocrity, not by nature, but, so to speak, by design, and from the beginning was expected to be indifferent to great moral challenges and unaware of the danger of a moral fall. Such was, more or less, the picture that the early modern thinkers created—mostly in opposition to the classical and Christian views of human nature—which, within a few centuries, managed to overcome virtually all of its competitors. Both regimes imagined man as a creature of common qualities whose commonness made him perceive the world through his own narrow vision and was therefore naturally inclined to reduce art, ideas, and education—contrary to the old view, which had attributed to them an elevating power—to his own dimensions.

I cannot refrain from making a personal note. The Poles could see the communist man in his full splendor during the early stages of communism, when, after having arrived on the Soviet tanks, he was enforcing the construction of the new regime in a society that had already been decimated and terrorized by the German occupation. A *homo novus*, uneducated, vulgar, primitive, having nothing but contempt for tradition, for the Polish imponderables, for history, culture, and anything subtle, genteel, elegant, beautiful, or spiritual, he was carrying out the destruction of social classes—the landed gentry, the middle class, the peasantry, the aristocracy, and even the working class whose interests he pretended to impersonate. He gave the Communist Party his will and his soul, and in return the party provided him with the formidable instruments of power as well as with what seemed to him the complete knowledge of the world. He did his job with a ruthlessness unmitigated by any inhibitions: Polish society underwent a profound and largely irreversible process of the destruction of culture. Life became boorish, social norms lost their force, and ugliness replaced beauty. One had an impression that the country fell into the hands of the barbarians. Later on, the communist man acquired some polishing, which did not touch his essence, but the damage could not be undone. This spectacular manifestation of Soviet barbarism—for which the Polish language had a lot of colorful expressions—was not a local phenomenon, but occurred in all the countries that came under communist rule.

When the communist order stabilized and the Soviet-type thugs retired or were pushed aside, there came a new generation of communists, no less vulgar than their predecessors but definitely not so brutal, presumably because of a fairly long period of peace. They expressed their desires in the communist newspeak that delineated the boundaries of their imagination and mental possibilities. Their lack of cultivation did not prevent them from having mastered a remarkable dexterity in moving within the intricate mechanisms of the communist bureaucracy, which was allotting privileges, benefits, property, and power.

The second time we encountered a wave of barbarism was immediately after the fall of communism. Naïve people thought that after the disappearance of the old regime a substantial part of the social fabric that it had destroyed would be restored and that freely elected governments and a liberated society would make an attempt to do so, or at least that the opening of the free space would boost—as it did during the first Solidarity period (1980–1981)—human energy to pursue the noble goals the old regime had debased. But whoever expected this was disappointed. Instead, we witnessed an invasion by another tribe of new men, boisterous and savage. The areas of freedom created by the crumbling of the old order became almost immediately occupied by the people coming—as it seemed—out of nowhere, in such great numbers that their victory was practically a Blitzkrieg.

Their strikingly loutish manners and coarse language did not have their origin in communism, but, as many found astonishing, in the patterns, or rather anti-patterns that developed in Western liberal democracies. Of course, the new order was different and had different mechanisms, but despite the differences it was directed against the social forms, types of conduct, norms, and practices to which the old order had been also hostile. Life underwent further vulgarization; the few practices and social norms that survived the previous invasion were subject to attacks by the new forces of barbarism; the ugliness of communist Poland did not disappear, and beauty was as much a rarity as it had been before. The new barbarians could hardly be called Bolsheviks or Soviet thugs, but there was something in their attitude that led to seeking similarities with their predecessors.

Their vulgarity was, so to speak, of the second order, as opposed to that which we had seen in communist Poland and which had had something primordial about it. What happened in the liberal democracy did not result from the absence of culture, and there was nothing natural about it; nor did it come from outside of the realm of civilization. In that, it differed from the vulgarity of the communists, who, before they captured power in Poland, had lived in environments practically unaffected by Polish culture. Having been long exposed to the Soviet influence, they felt an intense, instinctive antipathy toward the West as such, not knowing exactly what it was, and in particular for all forms of civilized conduct and propriety, which they thought both decadent and perfidious. The new barbarians of the liberal democracy, on the other hand, were products of the West, which at a certain stage of its history turned against its own culture; the respect for its achievements was gone, replaced by contempt, the rules of civility and propriety derided. To put it simply, the vulgarity of the communist system was precultural while that of liberal democracy is postcultural.

In both systems, man compensated for his commonness with the image of a large, well-functioning system: communism in one case and liberal democracy in the other, which, through the pursuit of collective goals—equality for all, peace, prosperity, etc.—released him from a necessity to aspire to the ideals that from the perspective of the political system might look redundant. It is therefore hardly surprising that just as "communism" (or "socialism") was the favorite word of the communist man, "democracy" has been such a word for the liberal-democratic man. The former liked to say "but in communism," "because in socialism," and suchlike, and the "argument of communism" was always the ultimate argument and by definition irrefutable. The latter loves saying, always with due piety mixed with a touch of audacity, "but in democracy" and "because in democracy," and the "argument of democracy" refutes all others. The number and frequency of the words "communism" (or "socialism") and "communist" (or "socialist") in the ancien régime are equal to the number and frequency of the words "democracy" and "democratic" in the new regime. The eagerness to use these words as trumps was not thought by the users to be a symptom of intellectual and moral capitulation, but rather, and quite sincerely, a manifestation of independence, courage, assertiveness, and autonomy. To a mediocre man, an organic assimilation with the system was the easiest way to develop a conviction of being exceptional.

Contrary to what many people think, the modern liberal-democratic world does not deviate much, in many important aspects, from the world that the communist man dreamed about and that, despite the enormous collective effort, he could not build within the communist institutions. There are differences, to be sure, but they are not so vast that they could be gratefully and unconditionally accepted by someone who has had firsthand experience with both systems, and then moved from one to the other.

It would not be, perhaps, inaccurate to say that the essence of the modern man's dream has come true, or, more modestly, that this process is still in progress. He has managed to divest himself of the major obligations that made his life difficult and is apparently planning to get rid of those that still remain. This sad state of affairs, however, does not make him despair. He is troubled neither by raging ideology that paralyzes his mind through stultifying stereotypes, nor by politicization, nor by the sterility of culture and the triumph of vulgarity. Even if he can notice all these regrettable developments and be sometimes annoyed by them, even if sometimes a thought passes through his mind that similar things happened in communism, he remains unperturbed and quickly convinces himself that replacing them with something else is impossible, and if it were possible, the results would be—for the reasons he does not bother to reflect upon—disastrous.

So the liberal democrats are quite right when they keep suggesting that the world has come to an end and that if it should continue to exist in a satisfactory way, it must be developed in the same vein. Of course, it is highly likely that some new rights will be invented to make everything yet more equal; that the feminist ideology and its spinoffs will prove to be even more absurd than before; that people who so proudly worship their intellectual independence will once again surprise everyone by meekly adopting it all. We can imagine a literature that will speak increasingly about nothing, and a diversity rhetoric even more raucous and more masking of the expanding uniformity. But all this will be yet another scene in the same final chapter of a long story that historically began in the early modern period, but that had its long *Vorgeschichte*. This chapter will include the fulfilment of what communism planned but what—to the immeasurable regret of its adherents—failed: namely, man's integration with the regime and the regime with man.

Whether the future of human history will add some new chapters, we cannot say, but such a scenario seems—upon the authority of common sense—likely. But the issue is not that new impulses, fashions, mood swings, major events, and other unpredictable factors will always emerge to affect the course of history and people's perception of it. The real change will come only when the current view of man spends itself and is considered inadequate. Only then will other stories develop or be revived—the former as a result of new experiences, the latter as a result of reactivating the long-dormant areas of collective memory—allowing a different look at human fate and the dreams through which individuals and communities express their aspirations. This course of events, surely, cannot be ruled out, although today the mere fact of considering it provokes anger and mockery by those who lost the habit of even contemplating such playful peregrinations of the human mind and feel a superstitious fear of leaving the secure territories of liberal-democratic orthodoxy.

But there exists yet another possibility. Perhaps the long story reaching denouement in its last chapter that modernity divulged to us is not just one of many stories that can be replaced by another, but a basic truth about modern man who, after many adventures, downfalls and ascents, exultations and tribulations, after following many chimeras and surrendering to many temptations, finally arrived at the accurate recognition of who he is. If this indeed were the case, then further fundamental changes in human history would no longer be possible, except changes for the worse. Such an eventuality would be, for some, a comforting testimony that man finally learned how to live in a sustainable harmony with his nature. For others it will be a final confirmation that his mediocrity is inveterate.